J 976.7 MCN
McNair, Sylvia.
Arkansas. $34.00

01/02

I0578940

DATE DUE

DE 31 02		
GAYLORD		PRINTED IN U.S.A.

Arkansas

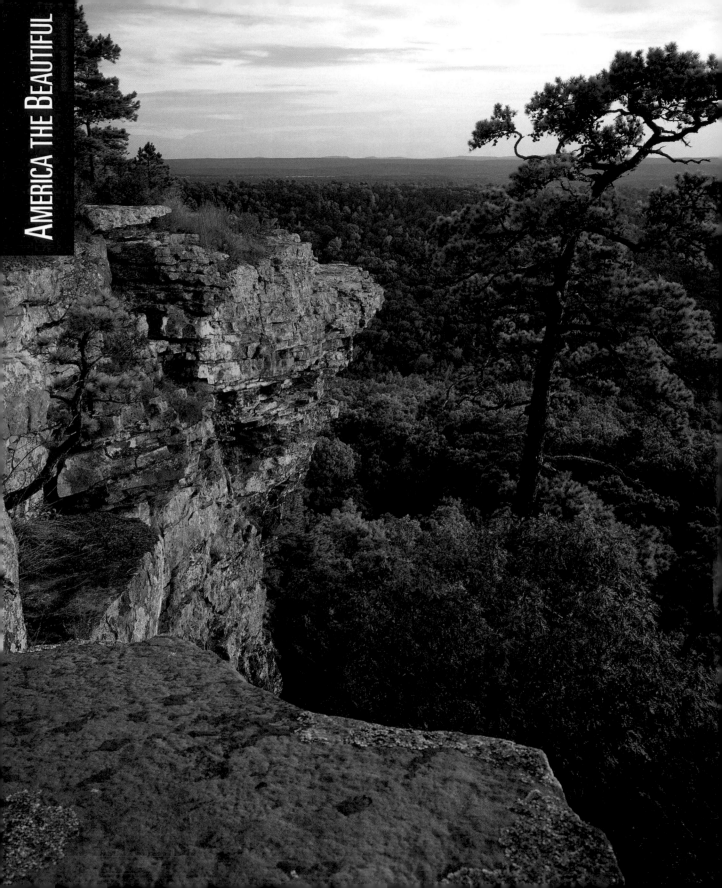

Arkansas

Sylvia McNair

Children's Press®
A Division of Scholastic Inc.
New York   Toronto   London   Auckland
Sydney   Mexico City   New Delhi   Hong Kong
Danbury, Connecticut

Frontispiece: Red Bluff in Petit Jean State Park

Front cover: Buffalo National River Trail in Newton County

Back cover: President Bill Clinton's birthplace

Consultant: Catherine Houser, Children's Library Program Adviser, Arkansas State Library

Please note: All statistics are as up-to-date as possible at the time of publication.

Visit Children's Press on the Internet at http://publishing.grolier.com

Book production by Editorial Directions, Inc.

Library of Congress Cataloging-in-Publication Data

McNair, Sylvia.
   Arkansas / Sylvia McNair.
      144 p. 24 cm. — (America the beautiful. Second series)
   Includes bibliographical references (p.) and index.
   Summary : Describes the geography, plants and animals, history, economy, language, religions, culture, and people of the state of Arkansas.
   ISBN 0-516-21089-0
   1. Arkansas—Juvenile literature. [1. Arkansas.] I. Title. II. Series.
F411.3.M37 2001
976.7—dc21

99-053361
CIP
AC

Acknowledgments

The author is extremely grateful to a number of Arkansas people who were most helpful in the preparation of this book. First of all, thanks to Tyler Hardeman, long-time friend, who introduced me to many corners of the state over a twenty-five year period. Hallie Simmins of Little Rock and Carolyn Neff of Hot Springs were most helpful in showing me their cities. Thanks to Kerry Kraus and Jim Taylor of the Arkansas Department of Parks and Tourism, who pointed me to many helpful sources of information. Thanks to both of them and to historian Dr. John L. Ferguson for reading the manuscript, correcting some errors, and making constructive suggestions.

And thanks to my personal editor and friend, Anna Idol, who is a whiz at catching most of my foolish errors before the manuscript goes to the publisher.

War Eagle Mill

Ozark Mountains

Buffalo River cliffs

Contents

Mockingbird

Sailing on Lake Ouachita

Little Rock

A young Arkansan

Scottie Pippen

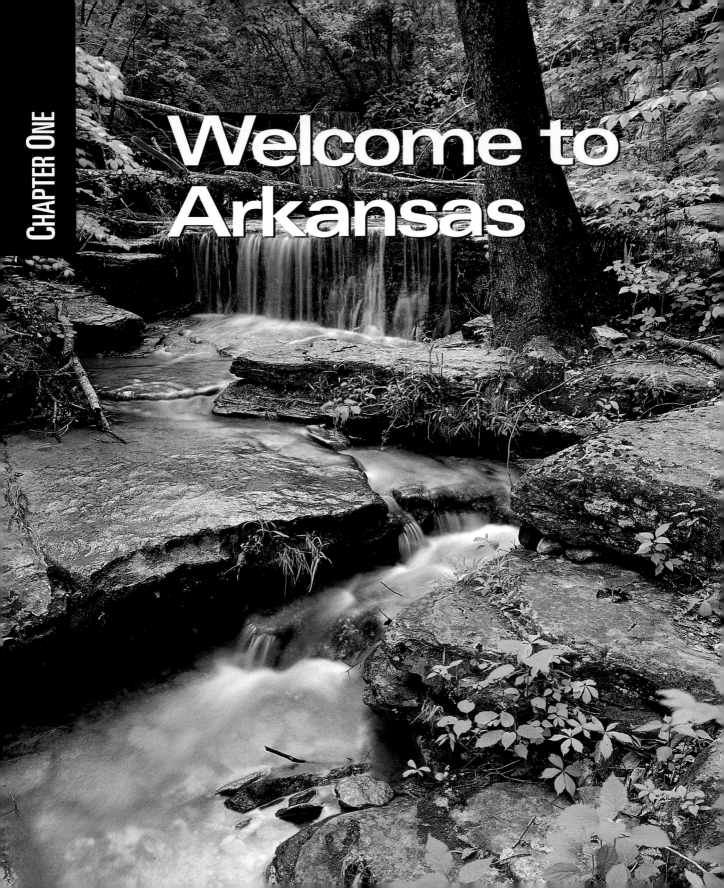

CHAPTER ONE

Welcome to Arkansas

How do you pronounce *Arkansas*? Is it AR-kan-SAW or Ar-KAN-sas? Do you pronounce the name of the state of Arkansas and the name of the Arkansas River the same way? The state legislature has made it official. Arkansas is always pronounced AR-kan-SAW. But the people who live here are usually called Ar-KAN-sans.

Only about 2½ million people live in Arkansas. Its cities are fairly small and surrounded by rural regions. Arkansans love their mountains, forests, rivers, lakes, and plentiful springs. This love is expressed in the state's nickname, which was chosen by the Arkansas legislature: The Natural State.

When European explorers and traders first came to the land west of the Mississippi River, they found three tribes of Native Americans in what is now Arkansas. The Osage roamed the Ozark Mountains in the north, hunting and trapping for food. The Caddo, in the south, and the Quapaw, in the east, were farmers who lived in small villages.

France claimed ownership of this land in 1682. Spain held it for a time, then France reclaimed it briefly. Then, in 1803, in one of the largest real estate purchases in history, President Thomas Jefferson acquired the Louisiana Territory for the young United States of

Most people in Arkansas live in either small towns or rural areas.

Opposite: Stairstep Falls along the Buffalo River

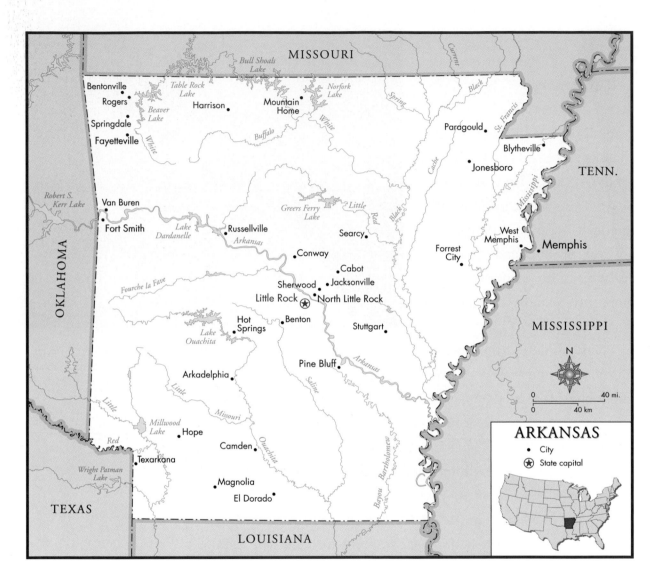

MISSOURI

Bull Shoals Lake

Bentonville

Rogers

Table Rock Lake

Springdale

Beaver Lake

Fayetteville

White

Harrison

Buffalo

Norfork Lake

Mountain Home

Spring

White

Robert S. Kerr Lake

Van Buren

Greers Ferry Lake

Little

Red

Black

Black

Currer

St. Francis

Paragould

Blytheville

Jonesboro

Cache

Mississippi

TENN.

OKLAHOMA

Fort Smith

Lake Dardanelle

Russellville

Arkansas

Searcy

Conway

Cabot

Sherwood
Jacksonville

Little Rock

North Little Rock

Hot Springs

Benton

Lake Ouachita

Fourche la Fave

Stuttgart

Arkansas

Arkadelphia

Little

Saline

Pine Bluff

Forrest City

West Memphis

Memphis

MISSISSIPPI

N

Millwood Lake

Hope

Missouri

Ouachita

Red

Texarkana

Wright Patman Lake

Camden

Bayou

Bartholomew

0   40 mi.
0   40 km

ARKANSAS

•   City

⭐ State capital

TEXAS

Magnolia

El Dorado

LOUISIANA

Geopolitical map of Arkansas

America. Included in that vast tract of land was present-day Arkansas.

Life in Arkansas has been difficult at times. In between long periods of mild weather, nasty tornadoes sometimes blow through the state. Once in a while, the rushing rivers so dear to fishers and canoeists overflow their banks, ruining farms and villages. And it isn't always easy to make a living in Arkansas, one of the poorest states in the Union.

But while some of the residents leave the state in search of greener pastures, others move in, attracted by the beauty and the relaxed, nature-oriented lifestyle. Let's explore Arkansas—its history, its land, and the people who have changed it from a little-known wilderness to a modern state.

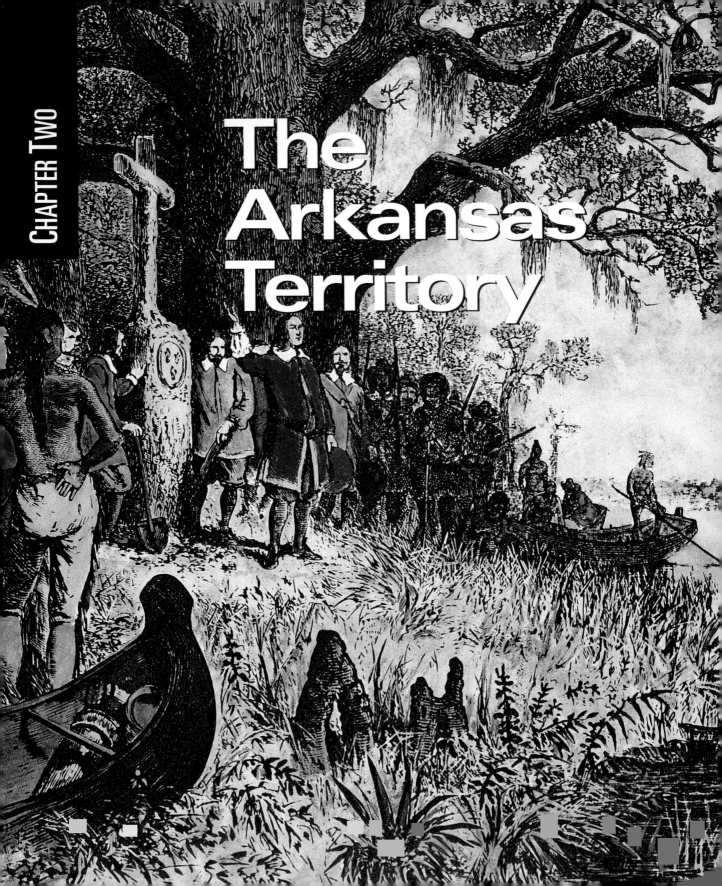

CHAPTER TWO

The Arkansas Territory

Some 12,000 years ago, huge prehistoric animals roamed the North American continent. Early humans made and used stone weapons and tools to hunt these animals. Some of the stone points made by Paleo Indians, as the archeologists call them, have been found in the Arkansas region. They were the first people in the area to leave any evidence that they existed.

Ancient mounds still exist at the Toltec Mounds Archaeological State Park.

The Archaic Period came next—after 10,000 B.C. Archaic Indians were a little more advanced. They used bark and grass to weave cloth and make baskets. Gradually, they began to raise crops for food and to live together in groups. As agriculture and craftsmanship developed, these groups started trading with one another.

By about 700 B.C., communities in the central part of North America built mounds. Some of these were burial mounds, where people were buried along with some of their possessions. Later mounds were used as platforms for ceremonies. One important

Opposite: La Salle proclaiming the French Empire in America

group of mounds can be visited today at Toltec Mounds Archaeological State Park, near Little Rock. Various groups of Native Americans lived in this area from about A.D. 650 to 1400.

The First European Exploration

When Christopher Columbus returned to Europe after his voyages across the Atlantic Ocean in the 1490s, he told of lands he had seen. Soon Spanish explorers and *conquistadors* (soldiers) were roaming all over the Caribbean Islands and North and South America. One of them, Hernando de Soto, took part in the conquest of Peru and served as governor of Cuba. From there, he decided to explore Florida in search of gold.

De Soto led his expedition across the southeastern part of North America. Near what is now Memphis, Tennessee, he spotted a large river. De Soto was the first European to cross the Mississippi, in 1541, and travel into present-day Arkansas.

De Soto and his soldiers traveled across the region. They found lowlands inhabited by scattered settlements of Native American farmers. Farther west, they found mountains and plains, and fewer people. De Soto and his men spent a few months exploring the region, then turned back to the Mississippi River. Before they could leave for Spain, De Soto died of a fever. His men buried him in the Mississippi.

Hernando de Soto on the shore of the Mississippi River

Soon people from European countries began to visit North America in increasing numbers. Spanish missionaries and conquistadors, hoping to find gold, concentrated on Florida and California. British immigrants started settlements in Virginia and New England. French hunters and trappers, called *voyageurs*, hiked through forests and paddled up and down rivers in the north. But no one paid much attention to Arkansas for the next 150 years.

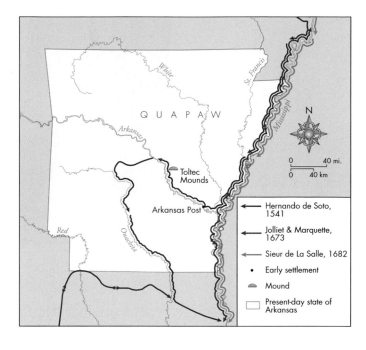

Exploration of Arkansas

The French Period

Two Frenchmen—Jacques Marquette, a Roman Catholic missionary, and Louis Jolliet, a fur trader—spent quite a bit of time in the northern wilderness. While exploring the area around the Great Lakes, they had heard of a great river nearby that flowed south. In 1673, they set out with a small group of voyageurs to explore that river. They hoped the river would take them to the Pacific Ocean.

The group paddled down the Mississippi as far as present-day Helena, Arkansas. From the Quapaw Indians, they learned that the river emptied into the Gulf of Mexico, not the Pacific Ocean. They were also warned that the Indians farther south were unfriendly. Besides, some of that territory was occupied by Spanish troops, and Spain and France were not on good terms. So the group turned back north with their maps and reports.

Jacques Marquette and Louis Jolliet exploring the Mississippi River in 1673

Marquette and Jolliet found a far smaller number of Native Americans than De Soto's expedition. Between the two explorations in Arkansas, something had wiped out many of the Native Americans living in the central part of the continent. Historians can only guess what happened. It may have been a drought, causing widespread starvation, or some kind of epidemic.

A French nobleman named René-Robert Cavalier, Sieur de La Salle, saw great potential in the fertile soil, lush forests, minerals, and fresh waters of mid-America and set out to explore the region. In 1682, he led a group of Indians, soldiers, and French adventurers down to the mouth of the Mississippi. There he claimed all the land drained by the Mississippi River and its tributaries for France and named the area Louisiana, in honor of the French king, Louis XIV.

La Salle returned to France and tried to interest the government in establishing settlements along the river. He was convinced that France could start a great empire in North America. Although few people paid any attention to him, he sailed back to the Americas,

Arkansas Post

A French adventurer named Henry de Tonty traveled with La Salle on the 1682 voyage down the Mississippi. The two men planned to meet again after La Salle's return from France. De Tonty traveled to the mouth of the Mississippi, but La Salle was stranded on the Texas coast.

"Iron Hand," as de Tonty was called because he had an artificial hand, went back north and traveled up the Arkansas River to a Quapaw village. He left half a dozen men there to establish the first European settlement in the lower Mississippi Valley. They named it Arkansas Post. Only a few soldiers, hunters, trappers, and occasionally a missionary or two, lived at Arkansas Post during its early years. Living conditions were difficult and primitive. Some of the men lived with Indian women and their children.

In 1819, when Arkansas became a territory of the United States, Arkansas Post was its first capital. In that same year, the first newspaper published west of the Mississippi River, the *Arkansas Gazette,* was founded here. Two years later, the capital—and the paper—were moved to Little Rock. However, Arkansas Post became a thriving community during the steamboat era and served as a strategic military fort during the Civil War.

In 1960, Congress named the site of Arkansas Post a national memorial. Arkansas Post Museum State Park, 3 miles (5 km) away, has five exhibit buildings with artifacts and documents depicting Arkansas history from colonial days to the present (above). ■

intending to establish a city at the mouth of the river. Unfortunately, his expedition overshot its destination and landed many miles west of the Mississippi.

During the French period, from 1682 to 1763, Arkansas Post was the only European settlement in the region. Occasionally, travelers dropped by the village on their way west, and a few French hunters and trappers passed through the surrounding wilderness.

The central part of North America claimed by France was huge, but the French government was too concerned with affairs in Europe to be bothered with trying to settle or develop its empire in North America. France was fighting a war against Britain and other nations in Europe, North America, India, southern Africa, and on the seas. These conflicts, called the Seven Years' War in Europe and the French and Indian War in North America, had little effect on the people in Arkansas. Eventually, France was defeated and forced to give up its claims in North America. Ownership of the Louisiana Territory then went to Spain.

Under Three Flags

The Louisiana Territory belonged to Spain from 1763 to 1800. Like the French before them, the Spanish paid little attention to this faraway territory. They established a governmental district, the District of Arkansas, with Arkansas Post as its center, but only about 200 Europeans lived there. A few Arkansans were vaguely aware that some of the British colonists in the northeast were engaged in a war. The Revolutionary War (1775–1783) had almost no immediate effect on the wilderness outposts west of the Mississippi River.

After the Revolutionary War ended, pioneers began traveling west in search of new lands and homes. Merchants and travelers saw a need to use the Mississippi River for transportation of goods and people. In 1795, Spain granted Americans the right to use the port of New Orleans.

In Europe, Napoleon Bonaparte of France was trying to build a vast empire. He forced the Spanish king to give the Louisiana Territory back to France in 1800, a fact that worried the young U.S. government. President Thomas Jefferson was concerned that Britain and France might go to war against each other. It that case, the two powers would almost surely fight over the port of New Orleans and the United States might be dragged into the conflict.

President Jefferson's ambassador to France, Robert Livingston, successfully negotiated a deal called the Louisiana Purchase with the French foreign minister. In this transaction, the United States acquired 828,000 square miles (2,144,520 square kilometers) of North American land for $15 million. That works out to less than three cents an acre (0.4 hectare)—one of the greatest real estate bargains in history. Overnight, the size of the United States was doubled.

Robert Livingston negotiated with France for the purchase of the Louisiana Territory.

The Arkansas Territory

The Louisiana Purchase was completed in 1803, and in the spring of 1804, the flag of the United States of America was raised over Arkansas Post. The Arkansas Territory was formed in 1819. The northern, southern, and eastern boundaries were the same as those of today's state of Arkansas, but the Arkansas Territory extended west over much of what is now Oklahoma and a little of the Texas Panhandle.

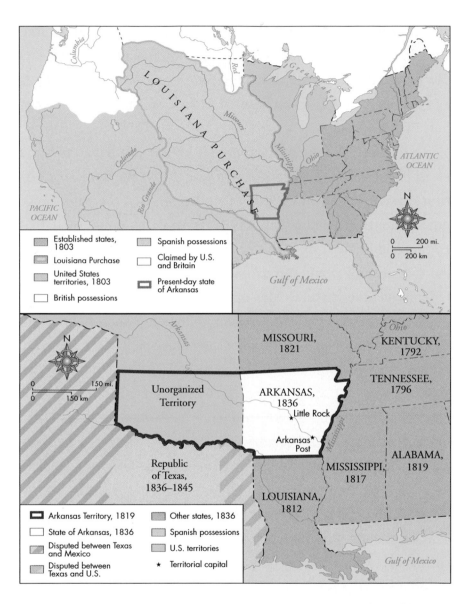

Historical maps of Arkansas

Legend (top map):
- Established states, 1803
- Louisiana Purchase
- United States territories, 1803
- British possessions
- Spanish possessions
- Claimed by U.S. and Britain
- Present-day state of Arkansas

Legend (bottom map):
- Arkansas Territory, 1819
- State of Arkansas, 1836
- Disputed between Texas and Mexico
- Disputed between Texas and U.S.
- Other states, 1836
- Spanish possessions
- U.S. territories
- ★ Territorial capital

The population of the new territory was about 14,000. Fewer than 1,000 Americans had lived there at the time of the Louisiana Purchase. For a short time, Arkansas Post was the territorial capital, but it was soon decided that a more central location would be

preferable. A capital city was planned near the "little rock," a well-known landmark on the Arkansas River. The capital was officially moved in 1821.

Life on a Frontier

The earliest Europeans in Arkansas were hunters who lived in one-room huts—log structures with dirt floors and no windows. The hunters lived as seminomads—loners who farmed a little but primarily lived on the game they hunted. Most of their clothing was made of deerskin. They trapped animals and traded the hides, along with wild honey, for salt, ammunition, blankets, cloth, and whiskey. There was no government to speak of and no law enforcement. They made their own rules.

By the time the Arkansas Territory was close to statehood, most of these frontiersmen were leaving for open country farther west. The people coming to the area planned to farm and raise fam-

ilies. They lived in much the same rough, simple way as the frontiersmen, but they had come to stay. They expected to build permanent homes and establish businesses and towns.

President Thomas Jefferson wanted settlers to make use of the vast expanses of western land in the Louisiana Purchase. He suggested that Native Americans in the eastern states should move west of the Mississippi River. Cherokee farmers were among the new settlers who came to Arkansas. Veterans of the War of 1812 were given titles to land as military bonuses. Others bought the land for as little as $1 to $3 an acre (0.4 ha). Still others were simply "squatters" who took over a piece of property and lived on it for years before filing a claim.

It was a hard life. They had to chop down and clear away the trees, plant crops, and wait for the harvest. In 1830, the average life expectancy was only thirty-five. Countless babies and children died of diseases such as measles, scarlet fever, whooping cough, bronchitis, pneumonia, tuberculosis, cholera, and typhoid. Mothers and infants often died in childbirth. There were no hospitals and few doctors. People suffered from poor nutrition. The settlers lived very far from one another, and there were no roads to connect them. Women did at least half the work on frontier farms, but they had no civil rights. They could not vote, own property, or make their own decisions.

Opposite: Building a log cabin

CHAPTER THREE

The Young State

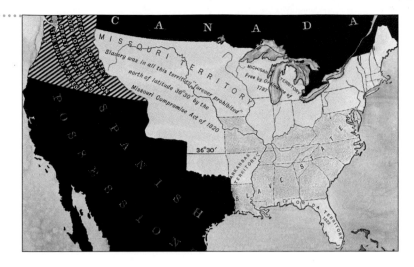

A map of the United States in 1820, showing slave states and free states

People in the Arkansas Territory were eager to establish a state of their own. The U.S. government had established rules for new states to enter the Union. First, the government would survey the land and set up land offices. Settlers could then buy parcels of land to live on. Money from these sales would be used to set up public schools and other facilities. The president would appoint a territorial governor. Next, residents of the territory could elect a legislature and send a non-voting delegate to the U.S. Congress.

When the citizens of a territory felt ready to organize a state, they could petition Congress for permission to write a state constitution. Once the constitution was approved, the territory would become a state. New states could enter the Union on an equal basis with older ones.

Ambrose H. Sevier was the delegate to the U.S. Congress from the Arkansas Territory. He petitioned Congress to grant the territorial legislature the right to prepare a state constitution. Even before gaining approval, the legislature completed the constitution and presented it to Congress. Shortly after that, on June 15, 1836, Arkansas was admitted to the Union as the twenty-fifth state.

In the U.S. Congress, trouble was brewing over the question of slavery. Slavery had been abolished in northern states. But in the South, large plantations dependent on slave labor were the back-

Opposite: Hot Springs in the 1870s

bone of the economy. Congress tried to keep a balance between the number of so-called free states and slave states. With the admission of Arkansas as a slave state and Michigan as a free state, the numbers remained equal.

But the controversy about slavery would grow more intense over the next few years. It would eventually tear the nation apart.

Early Years in the State

Only about 52,000 people lived in the new state of Arkansas, fewer than in many small cities of Arkansas today. But statehood attracted newcomers.

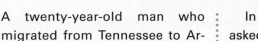

Ambrose H. Sevier

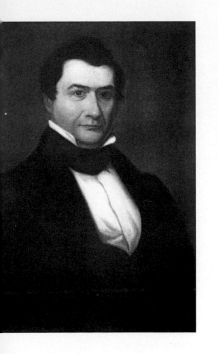

A twenty-year-old man who migrated from Tennessee to Arkansas Territory in 1821 became a leading power in early Arkansas politics. This man, Ambrose H. Sevier, was active both before and after Arkansas became a state.

Sevier began his career in the Arkansas Territory house of representatives. Later he became a member of the house, then its speaker. As territorial delegate to the U.S. Congress, he worked hard and successfully to win statehood for the territory. Then Sevier was elected one of Arkansas's first two U.S. senators.

In 1847, President James K. Polk asked Sevier to take on a special task. Sevier agreed, resigned from the Senate, and went to Mexico. As the president's representative, he helped negotiate the Treaty of Guadalupe Hildago, which officially ended the Mexican War (1846–1848). The treaty fixed the Rio Grande as the boundary between the United States and Mexico, thus adding a vast amount of territory to the United States. It included what are now the states of California, Nevada, and Utah; most of Arizona and New Mexico; and parts of Colorado and Wyoming. ■

The population of the United States was growing rapidly. Immigrants flocked to the United States from Europe. Jobs were plentiful in the factories of the Northeast, and cheap farmland was available in the new western territories.

Most of the state's newcomers came from other southern states. Eastern Arkansas was the fastest-growing region. The land in eastern Arkansas—the Mississippi Delta—is low and swampy. Farmers in this region were anxious to use this land to grow cotton. With some help from the federal government, they drained the wetlands and built levees to hold the river back. Cotton was the main crop, and slaves were used to plant, cultivate, and pick. Boats carried cotton down the Mississippi River to be shipped to textile mills.

By 1860, the state's population had grown to nearly half a million. About one-fourth of the people were slaves. Arkansas was sixth in the production of cotton in the nation.

Plantation owners relied on slaves to work in the cotton fields.

In the hill country, however, people were still quite isolated. Wagon roads that linked the towns were poor. Few farmers used machinery. Most grew only enough crops to feed their families, with a little left over to sell or trade for necessities. There were no hospitals, few schools, almost no stores, and not much law enforcement. There were churches, however.

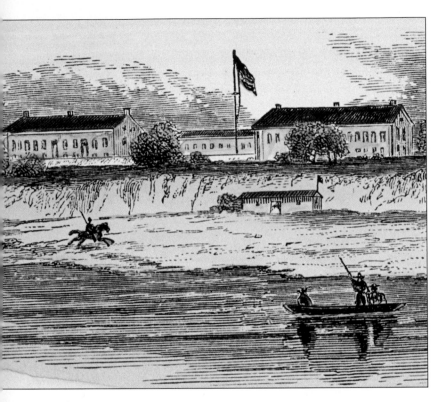
Fort Smith

The state had more than 1,000 of them by 1860.

Arkansas remained a frontier state for the rest of the century. More than half the land was still open. West of the state was Indian Territory, by treaty, until after the Civil War. Oklahoma did not become a state until 1907.

The United States went to war with Mexico in 1846. Although the population in Arkansas was still small, the state sent a regiment of 800 volunteers.

In 1849, Fort Smith became an important supply point for crowds of Forty-Niners—fortune hunters. They were on their way to California, where gold had been discovered.

Slavery and Politics

Arkansans were beginning to prosper by 1860. A financial panic that disturbed much of the United States in 1857 had little effect on Arkansas. And people of the state were barely aware of the turmoil over slavery that was brewing in other regions of the country.

The United States had divided into three major economies. Industry was the backbone of the economy in the Northeast. Farms producing food crops were the main source of income in the north-

County Names

Sixty of the seventy-five counties in Arkansas are named for individuals. Carroll County honors Charles Carroll, the last surviving signer of the Declaration of Independence. Two foreign heroes of the American Revolution were also commemorated: Pulaski County was named for a Polish soldier, and Lafayette County for the famous French supporter of the American cause. Various other war heroes, early settlers, and political figures appear on the list.

Benton County honors U.S. senator Thomas Hart Benton from Missouri, who helped achieve statehood for Arkansas. Sevier County remembers Ambrose Sevier, one of the first two senators from the new state. Cleveland, Grant, Jackson, Jefferson, Lincoln, Madison, Monroe, Polk, Van Buren, and Washington Counties were all named for presidents. ■

central states. And the economy of the southern states depended on large plantations, commercial farms producing mostly cotton.

Politically, the Democratic Party was the majority party in the South. Northerners, most of whom had been Whigs, were flocking to the new Republican Party.

Slavery had been abolished in most of the northern states by 1860. Antislavery movements were strong in these areas. And a serious rift was developing between the free states and slave states.

Southerners were concerned, because they believed their entire economy would collapse without slavery. However, the northern states had more than twice as many people. Southerners soon began to talk seriously about seceding, or withdrawing, from the United States. But the people of Arkansas were divided on the subject of secession.

Residents of the Mississippi Delta were solidly in favor of secession. The hill people in this state had almost no slaves, but they weren't necessarily opposed to the idea of slavery. Like people in the mountain areas of other southern states, they were independent, usually poor, loyal to the South, but not eager to secede from the nation.

The Civil War (1861–1865)

When the Republican candidate, Abraham Lincoln, was elected president, the government of South Carolina adopted an Ordinance of Secession. Five other states soon followed the lead, including two of Arkansas's neighbors, Mississippi and Louisiana. Arkansas hung back at first.

In January 1861, the legislature called for an election of delegates to a state convention to consider secession. The majority of those elected were generally pro-Union and hoped to find a compromise. The convention met on March 4, the day of Lincoln's inauguration. The delegates decided to let the people vote on secession in August.

But the die was cast in April, when the Confederate forces fired on Fort Sumter, in South Carolina. Lincoln considered this an act of war. The convention met again, adopted the new constitution of the Confederate States of America, and created the Army of Arkansas.

About 60,000 Arkansans served in the Confederate army during the war. Others—about 9,000 whites and 5,000 blacks—joined the Union army.

The bloodiest battle west of the Mississippi was fought in

The Battle of Pea Ridge was fought in 1862.

March 1862. In Pea Ridge, Arkansas, the Union army defeated the Confederates.

Ten months later, Arkansas Post surrendered to Union troops. This left the Arkansas River valley open. Northern troops entered Little Rock in September 1863. Two governments—Union and Confederate—operated in the state during the last year of the war.

Reconstruction

Arkansans suffered greatly during the war. Many people were killed or wounded. Hunger was widespread; food and medicines were scarce. Much of the northern half of the state was devastated. Homes were looted or demolished, banks and local governments were bankrupt, and inflation soared.

The period following the Civil War is called the Reconstruction Period. In 1867, Congress passed the Military Reconstruction Act, which divided ten of the former Confederate states into military districts, run by army officers. Strict requirements had to be met before a state could be readmitted to the Union. All former Confederate soldiers and office holders had to swear an oath of allegiance to the United States. The states had to write guarantees of civil rights into their constitutions and adopt the Fourteenth and Fifteenth Amendments to the U.S. Constitution. These amendments guaranteed civil rights to all citizens, including former slaves. Arkansas was readmitted to the Union in 1868.

Life in Arkansas gradually returned to normal after the Civil War. Cotton was still king in the delta, and the hill country remained pretty much a frontier.

Working the cotton press

Four kinds of farming existed in the state: cotton plantations, small family farms, subsistence farming, and sharecropping. A drought in 1881 and floods in 1882 spurred farmers to join self-help organizations, such as the Grange and the Agricultural Wheel.

Some small-scale industries appeared, such as sawmills, gristmills, and small factories making goods for local markets. But the Industrial Revolution that transformed life in other parts of the nation had little effect here.

Toltec Mounds

Native Americans who occupied the Mississippi Valley from A.D. 650 to 1050 were mound builders. Remains of a large ceremonial complex are preserved at Toltec Mounds Archaeological State Park, near Little Rock. Archaeologists have found many examples of fine pottery. In addition to jugs and pots, they found other pieces that were formed in the likeness of humans and animals. These pieces are called effigy vessels.

The Toltec site was first surveyed in 1891. Toltec Mounds got their name because of a probably untrue theory that the people who lived here might have been related to the Toltec people of Mexico.

It is one of the largest and most interesting Native American settlements in the lower Mississippi Valley. The visitor center has exhibits and audiovisual programs about the site's history and the archeological study still going on there. ■

The Progressive Era

Arkansas had, for the most part, recovered from the aftermath of the Civil War by the end of the nineteenth century. But it continued to be a poor state.

Historians have called the years from 1900 to 1920 in the United States the "progressive era." Reform movements were active in much of the country. People were working to improve education and health standards, make government more efficient, and increase public facilities and services.

In Arkansas, business and political leaders tried to help the state become more modern and prosperous. They recognized that education is an important key to progress and established a state board of education in 1909. New public high schools, teacher-training schools, and vocational schools were opened. Money to fund better education was always scarce, however.

The struggle for women's rights was an important issue of the time. In Arkansas, women could not own property or sign legal contracts. In 1915, the state legislature abolished these restric-

Many new public schools were built in the early 1900s.

tions. And in 1920, the U.S. Constitution was finally amended to give all female citizens the right to vote.

Despite some progress, several of the state's most important problems were left unsolved. Farm families—80 percent of the

"Jim Crow" Laws

The years following Reconstruction saw a renewal of racial prejudice. Many people, especially politicians, were afraid of the political power that black people were beginning to use in elections.

The so-called Jim Crow laws were passed in all the southern states and some midwestern states. These laws required separation of the races in public restrooms, restaurants, schools, colleges, and even in the use of drinking fountains. "Whites only" and "Coloreds only" signs were commonplace. Blacks had to ride on separate train cars and in the back of buses. They even had to use separate waiting rooms at bus and rail terminals. Special restrictions made it impossible for most African-Americans to exercise their right to vote, which was guaranteed by the Fifteenth Amendment.

In 1896, the U.S. Supreme Court ruled that it was constitutional for states to require separation of the races, as long as both groups were treated equally. The "separate but equal" argument stood for the next seventy years, even though it was obvious that the facilities and opportunities were always far from equal. ■

state's population—were still poor and in debt. Too many people depended on sharecropping for a living. Laws that promised protection of civil rights for African-Americans were not enforced. Second-class citizenship for blacks was a problem throughout the South.

World War I (1914–1918)

World War I broke out in Europe in 1914, and the United States joined the conflict in 1917. More than 70,000 Arkansans were in the armed services during the next year and a half. A major military training ground was established at Camp Pike, near Little Rock.

Shortly before the war ended, a deadly influenza epidemic spread through the country. Nationally, more lives were lost as a result of flu than in battle. The flu killed 7,000 Arkansans.

The end of World War I marked the beginning of a new age in the United States. Farming was shrinking in importance, and more and more people moved to cities to find jobs.

After World War I, many people in Arkansas left their farms to move to the cities.

CHAPTER FOUR

The Modernization of Arkansas

Postwar changes came more slowly in Arkansas than in many other parts of the United States, but they did come. A new industry—tourism—began to flourish in the 1920s. The automobile was a major factor. No longer dependent on rails and rivers for transportation, people discovered new places to visit—including Arkansas. Fishers, hunters, hikers, campers, and sightseers were delighted by the thousands of acres of unspoiled woods and waters in the Arkansas hill country.

Arkansans responded to the newfound popularity of their natural attractions. They built rental cottages and marked out scenic roads. The Ozark Playground Association was formed.

Another part of the state enjoyed a short but exciting burst of prosperity when an oil well near El Dorado began production in 1921. But most people in the state were still living in poverty.

Disaster struck in 1927, when horrendous floods on the Mississippi and its tributaries spilled over much of the state. Swirling waters broke through levees, destroyed crops, drowned livestock, tore out bridges, and forced more than 140,000 people to abandon their homes. No programs for federal disaster relief existed at that time. Only the Red Cross gave any help at all to the flood victims.

An oil well near El Dorado

Opposite: War Eagle Mill in springtime

The Great Depression

More disaster was to come. The floods were followed by a blisteringly hot and extremely dry year. The lowest rainfall in Arkansas history was recorded in 1930. Gardens and cotton crops were ruined. Farm incomes, already low, dropped to one-third of their former level.

The entire United States suffered through the Great Depression for the next decade. Cotton—once the mainstay of the state's agriculture—was selling for less than it cost to grow. Banks closed and many people lost their life's savings. Millions were out of work. Property was seized for nonpayment of taxes.

A major victim of the depression was education. Many towns simply didn't have enough money to pay teachers and keep the schools open.

In 1932, Arkansas became the first state to elect a woman to serve a full term in the U.S. Senate. In a special election held shortly after the death of her husband, Hattie W. Caraway was elected to the U.S. Senate. Also in 1932, Arkansans elected J. M. Futrell, a conservative Democrat, as governor, and they elected a Democratic president with quite different views.

Franklin Delano Roosevelt became president of the United States in 1933. He believed that the federal government should help people who could not help themselves. Among the programs in President Roosevelt's so-called New Deal were emergency relief, free school lunches, social security, price supports for farmers, soil conservation, and rural electrification. The Civilian Conservation Corps paid young men to plant trees on eroded land, establish fire

Senator Hattie W. Caraway

President Franklin D. Roosevelt helped states such as Arkansas with his New Deal programs.

roads through forests, and build or improve facilities in national and state parks.

Governor Futrell disapproved of all these measures, believing people could conquer poverty simply by working hard. The more money the federal government spent in Arkansas, the less Futrell wanted the state to contribute.

World War II (1939–1945)

As the depression ground on, war was brewing in Europe. Most Americans, especially in Arkansas, hoped the United States could avoid the conflict. But when the Japanese air force bombed Pearl Harbor on December 7, 1941, both the nation and the state became united behind the war effort overnight. A few people opposed the war on religious or philosophical grounds, but the overwhelming majority of Americans supported it.

Winthrop Rockefeller, a future governor of Arkansas, heading to army training camp in 1941

The war years brought more sweeping changes to Arkansas than any previous period. Workers flocked to the war plants that sprang up in El Dorado, Hope, Hot Springs, Little Rock, and other cities. Villages suddenly became boomtowns, and the new residents had difficulty finding housing. Unemployment disappeared in Arkansas in a few months, and soon there was a serious shortage of labor. People who had not held a job for years—if ever—joined the workforce. Blacks, women, and people on welfare went to work and proved to be capable and dedicated employees. Schools were hard hit again, as teachers joined the services or went to work in war plants.

Farm production and incomes soared. Wages were good and many consumer items were in short supply, so workers put their money into war bonds and savings accounts. Personal savings reached a new high.

Postwar Changes

Many changes came to Arkansas after the war ended. New roads were built. People moved around the state more than they had earlier. Large towns grew as small towns shrank or disappeared altogether. Public schools still suffered from a shortage of teachers though. One hundred schools in Arkansas closed in 1946. When schools and local stores closed, rural communities simply died out.

Arkansas gradually attracted some new industries. Factories relocated to the South. Unfortunately, many of the new jobs paid very low wages. Unions had never made much progress in organizing Arkansans, and manufacturers were able to find workers willing to work for low pay.

Government assistance, in the form of the G.I. Bill, made it possible for thousands of World War II veterans to get a college education. This was a mixed blessing for Arkansas, however, as many of their new graduates had to leave the state to find employment.

Crisis in Little Rock

Before the 1950s, most Americans knew very little about Arkansas. It wasn't the subject of best-selling books or popular movies. Its products were not household words. It simply wasn't a state that made headline news. But all that changed in 1957. Soon the whole world heard about Little Rock, Central High School, and Governor Orval Faubus.

Governor Orval Faubus showing a newspaper headline about the integration of Central High School in 1957

In May 1954, the U.S. Supreme Court made a decision that forever changed the relationship between people of different races in the United States. Ever since the first Africans had been brought to North America in slave ships, most white Americans had regarded them as inferior. Even otherwise compassionate, fair-minded people took racism for granted.

But the Supreme Court finally took a long, hard look at the principle of "separate but equal." For fifty-eight years, segregated schools had been considered constitutional as long as schools for blacks and whites were "equal." In 1954, the Supreme Court ruled that separate facilities were not equal and violated the Fourteenth Amendment to the Constitution. It further declared that segregation in public schools must be eliminated "with all deliberate speed."

Nothing changed in most of the southern states—for a while. Then a dramatic and stormy confrontation in Little Rock made headlines around the world. The story of the crisis is long and complicated. These are the facts in brief.

The Little Rock School Board wrote a plan to begin gradual desegregation of Central High School in September 1957. Nine African-American high-school students decided to enroll. They were college-bound students but they needed to attend certain courses that were not available in black schools.

Governor Orval Faubus, who was planning to run for a third term in office, was under pressure from segregationists. He tried to stall desegregation proceedings. When these efforts didn't work, he announced that he was calling out the National Guard to keep the black students from entering the school. He said it was being done to prevent violence, but he was defying the federal government. By his actions, he was saying that a state governor had more authority than the Supreme Court.

When the black students tried to enter the school on September 4, armed guards turned them back. The guards and angry mobs of segregationists kept the black students out of the school. Three weeks later, President Dwight Eisenhower intervened. He federalized the 10,000 members of the Arkansas National Guard and authorized the U.S. Army to send in an additional 1,000 troops. So, under armed protection, the nine students were permitted to attend school for the rest of the year.

That was not the end of the story, however. The atmosphere was tense in Little Rock for the rest of the school year. Inside the school, student bullies harassed the nine black students.

In 1958, the Arkansas legislature authorized the governor to close the high schools in Little Rock. Little Rock voters endorsed this action in a special election. During the year that the schools were closed, many white parents opted to send their children to private schools.

In 1959, public high schools were reopened by order of a federal court, and integration proceeded. Central High School has been declared a National Historic Landmark, and the National Park Service manages a small museum across the street from the school.

Federal troops escorting African-American students into Central High School

Daisy Bates

On August 22, 1957, in Little Rock, two weeks before Central High School's opening day, a rock was thrown through the front room window of the Bates home. Daisy Bates (above) was state president of the National Association for the Advancement of Colored People (NAACP) and co-owner of the *Arkansas State Press.* She and her husband were well known in Arkansas as an outspoken champions of civil rights for all, including blacks and women.

Bates was born and raised in a small, company-owned sawmill town in southern Arkansas. Adoptive parents brought her up because three white men had murdered her mother and her father had disappeared. She was awakened to the cruelty of discrimination when she was seven years old. Her adoptive father,

Two Courageous Women

however, taught her not to hate whites but injustice.

When she grew up, she married L. C. Bates, a journalist. They moved to Little Rock, where they saved their money and bought a weekly newspaper. The paper reported news of interest to the black community. The rock-throwing incident was a warning to them as black leaders, a threat that white segregationists would fight integration all the way.

Throughout the high-school crisis, Mrs. Bates met daily with the nine black students. She counseled them, encouraged them, and organized the black community to support and help them.

In 1962, Daisy Bates published a memoir of the Central High School story called *The Long Shadow of Little Rock.* Bates was honored many times in her later years for her civil rights work.

Adolphine Fletcher Terry

Adolphine Terry (above right) and her family were prominent white social and political leaders in Little Rock. Her father was a successful businessman and banker, and her brother, John

Gould Fletcher, was a Pulitzer Prize–winning poet. She was married to David D. Terry, who served in the U.S. Congress.

When Governor Faubus closed the Little Rock high schools in 1958, Terry wanted to do something. So she organized a group called the Women's Emergency Committee to Open Our Schools and held meetings in her home. The group recruited about 1,000 members, mostly white, well-educated women. They worked to defeat Governor Faubus by registering voters and arranging to transport them to the polls.

Terry graduated from a Little Rock high school in 1898 and Vassar College in 1902. In her will, she left her house to the city. In 1985, it was opened as part of the Arkansas Arts Center. ■

A Republican Governor

Orval Faubus was governor of Arkansas for twelve years. In 1967, Winthrop Rockefeller, the first Republican governor since Reconstruction days, succeeded him. Rockefeller was a wealthy New Yorker who had moved to an Arkansas mountaintop in the 1950s. He made a name for himself as a successful farmer, business executive, and philanthropist.

Winthrop Rockefeller became governor in 1967.

Rockefeller believed that Arkansas would be much better off with a two-party system, so he set about building up the state's tiny Republican Party. The Democrats tried to recruit him, but he decided to run for office as a Republican.

During his campaign, Winthrop Rockefeller conducted several public-opinion polls. The polls revealed that Arkansans preferred integration to racial strife. This fact was surprising, because the state's voters had repeatedly elected Governor Faubus, a man who had gained national recognition as a symbol of segregation.

When Winthrop Rockefeller was elected governor of the state in 1967, he drove out illegal gambling in Hot Springs. He tightened regulation of insurance and securities companies and improved public access to what was going on in state and local government. He also encouraged black voters to participate in Arkansas politics.

William Jefferson Clinton

William Jefferson Blythe IV was born in Hope, Arkansas, on August 19, 1946. His father was killed in an automobile crash before he was born. His mother later married Roger Clinton, and Bill Blythe's last name was changed to Clinton.

Bill Clinton grew up in Hot Springs. He was an excellent student and an all-state saxophone player. In 1963, he repre-sented Arkansas at Boys' Nation, in Washington, D.C. His experiences during the visit, especially meeting both Senator William Fulbright and President John F. Kennedy, stimulated his interest in politics.

Bill Clinton returned to Washington the following year to enter Georgetown University and work part-time for Senator Fulbright. He graduated with a degree in international affairs and won a Rhodes scholarship to study at Oxford University in England. From there, he went to Yale University Law School, where he met a fellow student named Hillary Rodham.

Both Clinton and Rodham joined the faculty of the University of Arkansas School of Law at Fayetteville. The two were married there in 1975. While in Fayetteville, Bill Clinton made his first run for public office (as U.S. representative) and lost. Two years later, he was elected attorney general of Arkansas. In 1978, Clinton was elected gov-ernor—the second-youngest person to hold that office in Arkansas history. He had a long list of legislative reforms he hoped to pass.

Republican Frank White de-feated Clinton when he ran for reelection as governor, but Clin-ton came back to be elected again in 1982, 1984, 1986, and 1990. (The term of office had been changed from two to four years by 1986.) The 1982 elec-tion campaign centered on the need to improve education in Arkansas, and the voters backed Clinton's platform. Bill Clinton's fellow governors voted him the most effective governor in the United States.

In 1992, Governor William Jefferson Clinton was elected president of the United States. In spite of allegations of scan-dals that tarnished his personal reputation, he completed a sec-ond term in office. ■

A solidly Democratic legislature prevented Rockefeller from carrying out all the reforms he wanted, however. He was defeated when he ran for a third term in 1970. Between 1970 and 2000, only two other Republican governors were elected: Frank White, who served from 1981 to 1983, and Mike Huckabee, who served from 1996 to 2000.

Governor Mike Huckabee

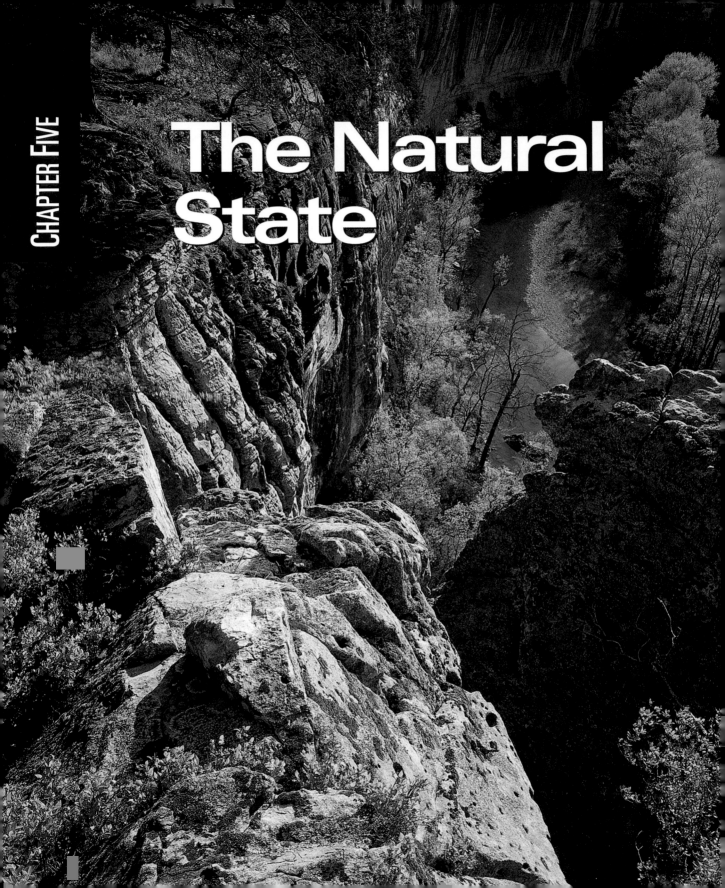

CHAPTER FIVE

The Natural State

W hat do the people of Arkansas love best about their state? Its natural beauty, without a doubt. The state's official nickname—The Natural State—appears on all the license plates, state government publications, and tourism posters. Although more than half the people in the state live in urban areas, nearly all of them spend most of their leisure time enjoying nature.

Arkansas license plates proclaim it "The Natural State."

Much of the land in the state is publicly owned and protected. If all the public lands were combined, the area would be larger than the state of Connecticut. Arkansas has fifty-one state parks, eighty-one wildlife management areas, three national forests, a national river, and a national park.

Land Forms

If natural features determined state boundaries, Arkansas would be divided into two states. The line between them would start on the northern border, about 30 miles (48 kilometers) west of the Mississippi River. From there, the line would run in a generally southwesterly direction through Little Rock and on to De Queen and the Oklahoma border. West and north of the line are highlands, a rugged region of mountains, gorges, and thin, rocky soil. East and south are flat and fertile lowlands, covered with rich bottomland.

Opposite: Buffalo River cliffs in the Ozark Mountains

Cassatot Falls in the Ouachita Mountains

Within these types of land are five subdivisions. The highlands are made up of the Ozark Plateau (also called the Ozark Mountains), the Arkansas River valley, and the Ouachita Mountains. The Ozark and Ouachita Mountains are the only major ranges between the Rockies and the Appalachians. The lowlands include the Mississippi River alluvial plain and the West Gulf Coastal Plain. Little Rock, in the center of the state, is at the meeting point of the five geographical subdivisions.

A view of the Ozark Mountains

Geographic Facts

Arkansas, in the south-central United States, is shaped roughly like a trapezoid—a four-sided figure with two parallel sides. The northern and southern borders are straight and parallel. Missouri is on the north, Louisiana on the south. The western border, with Oklahoma, is nearly straight until it reaches the Red River, in the southwestern corner of Arkansas. At this point, a small corner of the trapezoid belongs to Texas. Up in the northeast, another corner is part of Missouri.

The eastern border of the state originally followed the Mississippi River, but the river has changed its course in various spots. As a result, small pockets of Arkansas land are now in the states across the river (Mississippi and Tennessee) and bits of those states are now in Arkansas.

Arkansas, with a total area of 53,183 square miles (137,744 sq km), ranks twenty-eighth in size among the fifty states. Its greatest distance is 240 miles (386 km) from north to south, and 276 miles (444 km) from east to west.

Summers tend to be extremely hot and humid, especially in the lowlands. Winters are generally mild with occasional cold snaps. The state enjoys a long growing season with plenty of rain. Droughts are rare in Arkansas. ■

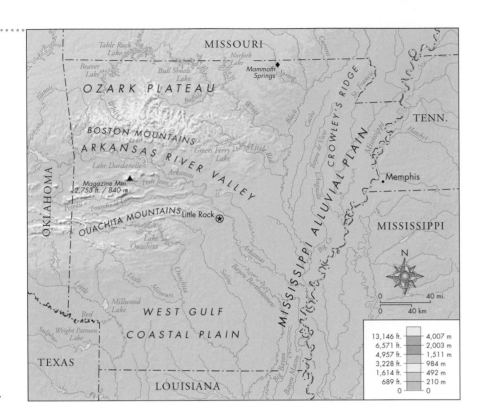

Arkansas's topography

Arkansas's Geographical Features

Total area; rank	53,183 sq. mi. (137,744 sq km); 28th
Land; rank	52,076 sq. mi. (134,877 sq km); 27th
Water; rank	1,107 sq. mi. (2,867 sq km); 25th
***Inland water*; rank**	1,107 sq. mi. (2,867 sq km); 18th
Geographic center	Pulaski, 12 miles (19 km) northwest of Little Rock
Highest point	Magazine Mountain, 2,753 feet (840 m)
Lowest point	55 feet (17 m) above sea level at Oachita River
Largest city	Little Rock
Population; rank	2,362,239 (1990 census); 33rd
Record high temperature	120°F (49°C) at Ozark on August 10, 1936
Record low temperature	−29°F (−34°C) in Benton County on February 13, 1905
Average July temperature	81°F (27°C)
Average January temperature	40°F (4°C)
Average annual precipitation	49 inches (124 cm)

Tornadoes

Tornadoes are common in many midwestern states, especially in the Mississippi Valley. The twisters that hit Arkansas are often extremely severe. One storm in 1952 killed 111 people and injured hundreds of others.

Also called cyclones, tornadoes often accompany thunderstorms. A dark funnel may be seen hanging down from a dark cloud. If it touches the ground, it can travel along, carrying powerful whirlwinds with it. These whirling winds can pick up heavy objects—even entire buildings—and toss them through the air with great force. In Arkansas, most severe tornadoes occur from March through September, usually in late afternoon and evening. ■

The Ozarks

The Ozark Plateau is a large region in the south-central United States, stretching through parts of Illinois, Missouri, and Oklahoma as well as Arkansas. It covers most of northwest and north-central Arkansas. Its rugged beauty consists of tree-covered mountains, deep gorges, flat-topped ridges, and multicolored bluffs of limestone and sandstone. Water is abundant, in the form of waterfalls, springs, rivers, streams, and lakes. Underground are caves and caverns to be explored. Blanchard Caverns, near Moun-

Blanchard Caverns is a large system of caves.

tain View, is one of largest cave systems in the United States. It has spectacular formations, an underground river, and huge open chambers.

Springs spout from Ozark hillsides and bubble up from the ground to form pools. Mammoth Springs, on the Missouri border in eastern Arkansas, is one of the largest in the world, producing some 200 million gallons (757 million liters) per day. Farther west lies Eureka Springs, a town that is famous for its sixty-three mineral springs. Native Americans used to camp in this area because of its abundant supply of water. In the 1880s, white people heard that these springs had miraculous healing powers. Many traveled long distances, hoping to find a remedy for various ailments.

The Ozark National Forest covers more than 1 million acres (405,000 ha) of land, including five wilderness areas and six wild and scenic rivers. Three large lakes—Beaver, Norfork, and Bull Shoals—are popular spots for fishing and other water sports. In general, the land in this region is not good for crops, but a few

Buffalo National River

All the rivers in Arkansas drain into the Mississippi River. They were important waterways for the Native Americans and early white settlers. The Buffalo River (right) begins in northwestern Arkansas and flows eastward to join the White River, which proceeds south to the Mississippi.

The Buffalo is one of only a few rivers in the United States that is still free-flowing—its course has not been altered by the construction of dams. In the 1950s, the U.S. Army Corps of Engineers had plans to build a dam on it, but conservationists objected strongly. Congress listened to the objections and passed a law in 1972 making the Buffalo the nation's first national river. The law protects the stream from any further development and allows it to continue in its wild and scenic state. In 1978, much of the land along both banks of the river was designated as wilderness.

Recreational opportunities on the river and its shores are great. Visitors come to hunt, fish, hike the wilderness trails, ride the rapids of the upper river, or float peacefully through pools in its quieter spots.

Wildlife native to the Ozarks includes more than 200 species of birds and 59 kinds of fish, as well as deer, squirrels, bobcats, foxes, coyotes, and black bears. A recent program has reintroduced elk to the region and a herd of about 500 now enjoy the wilderness along the Buffalo National River. ■

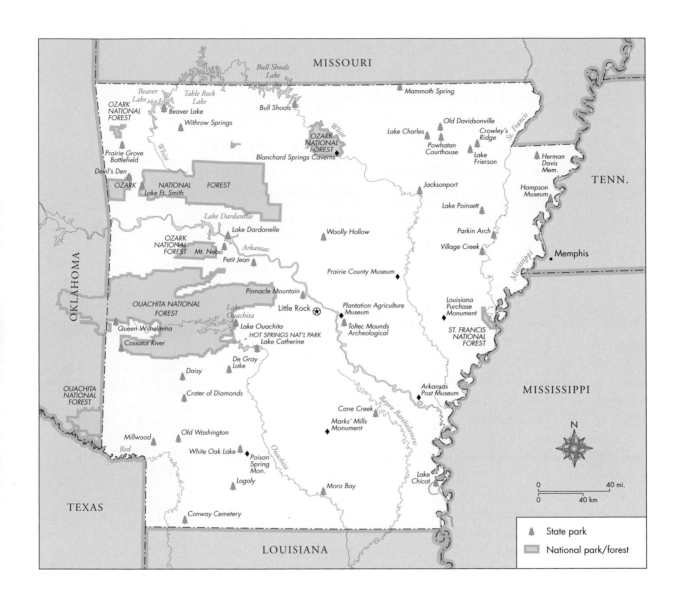

Arkansas's parks and forests

herds of cows graze on its scattered pasturelands, and its peach orchards are heavy with fruit in late summer.

Spring in the Arkansas highlands turns the hillsides into a dazzling bouquet of white flowering dogwoods, dark pink redbuds, and

wild azaleas. Hardwood trees are just beginning to unveil their soft green new leaves. Azaleas set the underbrush ablaze with color. Summer is usually lush and green. In autumn, brilliant crimson sumac bushes accent the changing colors of hardwood trees.

Wildflowers in Petit Jean State Park

Arkansas Valley

The Arkansas River, the fourth-longest river in the United States, takes a tumultuous trip from its source in the Colorado Rocky Mountains to the state that shares its name. Swift and wild as it tumbles down the slopes and races through the gorges in Colorado, it gets wider and more peaceful as it courses through Oklahoma.

A view of the Arkansas River

In Arkansas, the river cuts between the Ozark and Ouachita Mountains, creating a broad, rolling valley. The Arkansas Valley is considered part of the highlands, though most of it is lower in elevation than the regions on either side of it. However, several peaks rise from the valley floor including Magazine Mountain, the highest point in the state at 2,753 feet (840 m).

A series of eighteen dams in Oklahoma and Arkansas has tamed the frisky Arkansas River to make barge traffic possible. Many parks and campgrounds lie along its shore. The Arkansas

Who Was Petit Jean?

Petit Jean Mountain is somewhat of a mystery. Not really a part of either the Ozark or Ouachita Ranges, it rises alone at the eastern end of the Arkansas Valley.

An old legend says the mountain was named for a young Frenchwoman who was in the region in the early 1700s. She is said to have disguised herself as a boy to get a job on a ship that was exploring the Louisiana Territory. Her boyfriend was on board, and she wanted to be with him. Because she was small, her shipmates began to call her *Petit Jean* (Little John).

Tragically, the young woman became fatally ill with a fever. Her secret was revealed before she died. According to the legend, friendly Native Americans buried her on the side of the mountain. Local residents have cared for a gravesite thought to be that of Petit Jean for many years. A black wrought-iron fence protects it.

Petit Jean State Park (right), developed in the 1930s by the Civilian Conservation Corps, was the first park in the Arkansas state park system. Its log and stone buildings are set amid rugged bluffs, waterfalls, caves, springs, and a scenic canyon. It is one of the most beautiful parks in the state. ■

River is one of the world's most productive fish habitats. Deposits of coal and natural gas lie under fertile plains and pastures in the wide valley on either side of the river.

The Ouachitas

Almost all mountain ranges in North America run north and south. Only the Ouachitas (pronounced WASH-i-taws) in Arkansas run east and west. Some scientists think these mountains might have once been part of the Appalachians. Others believe they were pushed up from the ocean floor some 300 million years ago by a collision of landmasses.

The Ouachita Mountains rise in west-central Arkansas between the Arkansas Valley and the West Gulf Coastal Plain. Not many people live in this region of tall ridges and tree-covered slopes. Much of it is within the Ouachita National Forest. Lake Ouachita, the largest artificial lake in Arkansas, is full of bass, catfish, and other species. Several other lakes have equally beautiful settings in the midst of the tree-covered mountains. The Ouachitas attract thousands of campers, fishers, and weekending families. Hikers enjoy exploring the 223-mile (359-km) Ouachita Trail. Five wilderness areas and two wild and scenic rivers provide an ideal habitat for many species of wildlife.

The Ouachita Mountains run east and west.

Winters in the Ouachitas are mild but summers can be extremely hot. These mountains don't get much snow, though they experience occasional ice storms. Spring splashes the woods and pastures with wildflowers.

Seventy-five kinds of minerals have been found near Hot Springs. Fuel sources include petroleum, natural gas, and lignite.

Opposite: Sailing on Lake Ouachita

From Arrowheads to Dentists' Drills

Paleo-Indians, the ancestors of today's Native Americans, lived in Arkansas several thousand years ago. They were hunters and gatherers who fashioned tools out of a stone called novaculite (above). This stone is much harder, and better for toolmaking, than any other.

The early Arkansas Indians discovered that heating a piece of this very hard stone in a fire pit made it flakier and easier to chip and shape into tools. After the stone was tempered in this way, the toolmakers sliced it into slabs and used elk or deer horns to rough out a piece. Next they began to tap at the edges of the stone. This tedious process, called "napping," flakes away slivers of stone, leaving a thin, sharp point. Native Americans used points of various sizes for arrowheads, knives, and scrapers. They traded their points with other natives. Archaeologists have found points made of Arkansas novaculite in places that are hundreds of miles away from the source of the stone.

Today, novaculite is mostly used to make sharpening stones called whetstones. They are used to sharpen dental drills, surgical instruments, and all kinds of precision-cutting tools. The rocks are still heat-treated, or tempered, just as they were during the Stone Age.

Dan's Whetstone Company, near Hot Springs, is a small, family-run company. A few workers do all the quarrying, tempering, sizing, and shaping of novaculite. Much of the work is done by hand. Tool manufacturers all over the world buy whetstones from this company.

One member of the family has had an interesting hobby ever since he was a child. In his spare time he is a "whetnapper." He uses the same method as the first people of Arkansas to create points and knives. ■

Among the metals are bauxite, iron ore, zinc, manganese, and silver. Significant deposits of sandstone, marble, gypsum, asphalt, and quartz crystals are also found there.

Arkansas is North America's only major source of novaculite, an extremely hard stone. Sometimes it contains traces of manganese, carbon, and iron, which create a variety of colors and shapes, like pictures in the stone.

The West Gulf Coastal Plain

A huge plain extends along the coast of the Atlantic Ocean and the Gulf of Mexico. In Arkansas, the West Gulf Coastal Plain extends from the Ouachita Mountains south to the Louisiana border. A land of gently rolling hills and streams bordered with lowlands, it includes most of the southwestern and south-central parts of the state.

The lowest point in the state—55 feet (17 m)—is near where the Ouachita River flows into Louisiana. Much of the area is thickly covered with pine forests, and lumbering is a major industry. Winters are mild in southern Arkansas. An occasional cold snap may bring down the temperature, but usually for just a short time.

Riches have been found underground in this region. The only diamond mine open to the public in the United States lies at the northern edge, where the Ouachita Mountains give way to the coastal plain. In the early 1900s, the discovery of oil and natural gas turned the southern village of El Dorado into a boomtown. Southern Arkansas has no major cities. The people live in small, scattered towns and villages, and small farms produce livestock, poultry, fruits, and vegetables.

Fishing on Little Red River

Fishing is exceptionally good in the rivers that run through the coastal plain. The riverbanks are almost entirely untouched by development, and fishers can float along in an atmosphere that seems miles away from modern civilization.

The beauty of the Gulf Plain is subtle and quiet, not like the dramatic vistas in the mountains. Lush creeks and swamps run through grassy glades and cypress swamps. White-tailed deer, wild turkey, quail, and a large variety of songbirds make their home in the backcountry.

The Delta

The geographic name for the landform that makes up the eastern third of Arkansas is the Mississippi Alluvial Plain, but most people call it the delta. The entire Mississippi Delta extends more than 15,000 square miles (38,850 sq km) in the states of Missouri, Kentucky, Tennessee, Arkansas, Mississippi, and Louisiana. The soil of a delta is alluvial—made of clay, silt, and sand deposited by running water.

The Mississippi River forms most of the eastern boundary of Arkansas. Flooding, receding, and wandering of the rivers over thousands of years created the delta. The landscape frequently changes as streams shift courses. Every flood washes away land in some areas and builds it up in others.

Most of the natural lakes in Arkansas are oxbows. An oxbow

The New Madrid Earthquake

The greatest natural disaster in the history of the Arkansas Territory began on December 16, 1811. The New Madrid Earthquake was given that name because the closest settlement to the quake at that time was New Madrid, Missouri. Actually, it was a series of earthquakes—some sources say more than 1,800—over a period of three or four months. At least six major quakes in the region had been reported during the previous 112 years. Some may have been even more powerful than this series.

The tremors began along the St. Francis River in Arkansas. Regions of Tennessee and Arkansas were most affected. The Mississippi River changed its course, creating Reelfoot Lake in Tennessee. The quakes also raised the elevation of Crowleys Ridge.

At that time, very few people lived in the area of greatest damage (right), so we have few first-hand accounts. If a major earthquake were to erupt along the New Madrid fault line today, it could wipe out the cities of Memphis, Tennessee, and Jonesboro, Arkansas. Levees could be destroyed all along the Mississippi, resulting in major floods and the loss of many lives. ■

lake is created when a river changes its course. Lake Chicot, the state's largest natural lake, a huge oxbow formed by the Mississippi, is near the southern border.

The state's major agricultural products are raised in the rich land of the delta. An extensive system of levees and drainage ditches has been built to give some protection from flooding, but every once in a while the mighty Mississippi proves that human efforts have not really tamed its waters.

Before settlers began to change the landscape of Arkansas, the delta consisted of huge, wild swamps along the river and tall-grass prairies to the west. Forests of tupelos, cypress trees, and towering oaks grew in the swamps. Deer and black bears roamed the region.

Crowleys Ridge

The Mississippi Delta is almost entirely flat, with one mysterious exception. A long strip that looks completely out of place runs north and south for 150 miles (241 km) through the delta, from southern Illinois and Missouri to Helena, Arkansas. It is from 1 to 10 miles (1.6 to 16 km) wide and from 200 to 300 feet (61 to 92 m) high. Two rivers slice through the ridge.

Crowleys Ridge (above) is sometimes called a sixth Arkansas landform, because it is so different from the delta that surrounds it. In contrast to the alluvial soil of a delta, the ridge is covered with loess—a yellow and brownish combination of topsoil and bits of minerals blown in by the wind. The cool breezes that brush through the tall pines here offer a welcome change from the constant heat and humidity of summers in the delta.

Two lakes, a small national forest, and a state park are located in Crowleys Ridge. ■

Today most of the delta is plantation country. Cotton, soybeans, wheat, and especially rice grow in fertile soil that is several feet deep. Orchards have rows of pecan trees. Some farms have commercial "aquaculture" ponds, stocked with catfish and crawfish.

**Arkansas has many
hardwood forests.**

The Mississippi is a flyway for millions of ducks and other migratory waterfowl. A dozen wildlife-management areas and national wildlife refuges have been created to preserve the natural habitat these creatures depend on.

CHAPTER SIX

Here and There in Arkansas

n Arkansas, all roads lead to Little Rock, the political and geographical hub of the state. Little Rock sits on the south bank of the Arkansas River, facing its sister city, North Little Rock, across the water. At this point, the Arkansas River leaves the highlands to flow across the delta to the Mississippi.

The early days of Little Rock are commemorated in several preserved and restored buildings. The recently renovated Old State House, the state's capitol from 1836 to 1911, is now a historical museum. A few steps away stands a group of some of the oldest buildings in the city—an outdoor museum called the Arkansas Territorial Restoration. Arkansas's state capitol, used since 1911, is a replica of the Capitol in Washington, D.C., three-fourths the size of the original.

Little Rock is the largest metropolitan area in Arkansas.

Opposite: Riverfront Park in Little Rock

The Old State House
in Little Rock

Both visitors and residents like to walk along the river in River-front Park. The nearby River Market houses a public library, shops, restaurants, and the Museum of Discovery. In summer, people can enjoy river cruises, outdoor festivals, and Arkansas Travelers baseball games. The fall and winter seasons bring symphony concerts and theatrical performances.

Little Rock Central High Museum interprets the unfortunate events of 1957 in a clear and impartial manner. A new museum of military history, built in an old arsenal structure, is named for Arkansas native General Douglas MacArthur. Mountains, lakes, natural springs, caves, and forests—all the wonders of nature—surround Little Rock.

The Ouachitas

Less than 50 miles (80 km) west of Little Rock lie the Ouachita Mountains and the number-one tourist attraction in the state. Hot Springs is the name of both a city and a national park—and a per-

Hot Springs National Park

Native Americans told early explorers and settlers about a valley in the Ouachita Mountains where dozens of springs poured out hot water. Their ancestors had been visiting the area for thousands of years. Legend says that Hernando de Soto may have seen the hot springs in 1541.

Early American explorers wrote descriptions of steaming hot water gushing out of a rocky hillside in a region surrounded by mountains. The mineral waters had shaped and colored the rocks so that they looked like the inside of a cave.

In 1832, Congress set aside four sections of land in a reservation. This was the first area in the nation to be protected in this way. So, in a sense, Hot Springs was the first U.S. national park, though it was not officially declared a national park until 1921.

A village grew up around the reservation and hot mineral baths were offered in several buildings that still stand along Bathhouse Row (above). The National Park Service runs a small museum and gift shop in one of these historic structures while hot baths and massage treatments are available in another. Most of the forty-seven springs have now been covered over to prevent contamination. One beautiful cascade tumbles over rocks in the center of town, across the street from the Arlington Hotel, giving an idea of what the area looked like before people started living there. ■

son can't really tell which is which. The park is largely inside the city and part of the city is inside the park.

Early in Arkansas history, people began visiting the thermal waters of Hot Springs. They had heard that bathing in the hot springs cured people of various ailments—or at least made them feel a lot better. In 1832, the government established Hot Springs Reservation to protect the springs.

After the Civil War, the fame of Hot Springs spread around the world. Luxury hotels soon appeared, and Bathhouse Row became the downtown of a growing village. In the 1920s and 1930s, people with less healthy interests discovered Hot Springs. Gambling casinos and betting parlors flourished here. Gangsters came from the big cities to take the waters—and the gamblers' money. Illegal gambling continued until the 1960s, when a reform-minded state administration shut down the casinos.

The discovery of antibiotics made people less reliant on thermal springs for healing. Hot Springs declined as a tourist destination, and city businesses started to deteriorate along with the historic bathhouses.

In the late 1980s and 1990s, things began to turn around, however. Downtown has been restored as a historic district, and the hotels are busy again. Attractive shops, excellent restaurants, fine art galleries, special festivals and events, and family entertainment have given new life to both the city and the park.

Southwest of Hot Springs, at the southern edge of the Ouachita Mountains, is the only park of its kind in North America. Owned by the state of Arkansas, Crater of Diamonds State Park is open to the public. Visitors can rent digging tools and try their luck at rock

hunting. People of all ages have fun trying to find the precious gems, and finders are keepers. Park personnel identify, grade, and weigh the stones.

Digging for diamonds at Crater of Diamonds State Park

More than 70,000 diamonds have been found here since the state park was established in 1972, and some of them were extremely valuable. Other precious stones are found, too, such as amethysts and garnets.

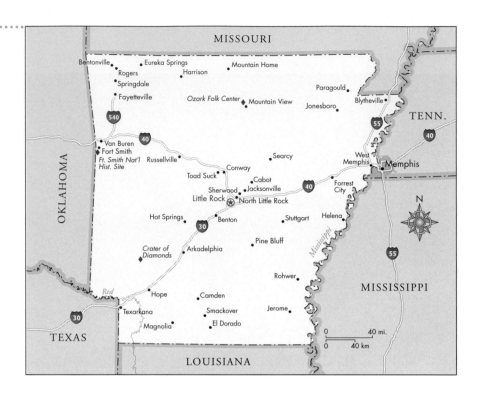

Arkansas's cities and interstates

Arkansas River Valley

The Arkansas River valley between Little Rock and Fort Smith lies between the Ouachita and Ozark Mountains. At the Oklahoma border, where the Arkansas River enters Arkansas, stands Fort Smith, once a wild and woolly frontier settlement.

Fort Smith was built in 1817 as a military outpost. When Arkansas became a state, its western boundary was drawn just west of the fort. By that time, the garrison was used primarily as a supply depot for other forts west of it. When gold was discovered in California, the town became a supply depot for fortune hunters traveling west.

Confederates troops seized the fort early in the Civil War. The fort changed hands between Union and Confederate forces several times, but no major battles were fought here.

Fort Smith National Historic Site

In 1875, Isaac C. Parker, the "Hanging Judge," arrived in Fort Smith to take over the Western District Court and establish law and order. This was a real frontier town. It bordered on Oklahoma Territory, which did not become a state until 1906. Murderers, train robbers, and other desperadoes roamed the territory to the west. Parker presided over thousands of cases. He was nicknamed the "Hanging Judge" because seventy-nine convicted criminals were hanged during his years on the bench.

Fort Smith's turbulent past is commemorated at the Fort Smith National Historic Site, on a bluff high above the Arkansas River. The site includes the remains of two fort buildings, Judge Parker's court, and a reproduction of the jail and of the 1886 gallows. ■

Toward the end of the nineteenth century, Fort Smith began to change from a frontier post into a city. Its location on the Arkansas River and close to sources of coal and natural gas made it an ideal spot for factories. Today, Fort Smith is a leading manufacturing center.

The Ozarks

Fayetteville's settlers believed in education and were determined to have good schools. One important early school, Fayetteville Female Seminary, was founded by Sophia Sawyer, a missionary to the Cherokee. Sophia's interest in teaching Cherokee girls as well as the daughters of white settlers made her unpopular with some of the townspeople.

Several small colleges were established here in the 1840s and 1850s. Arkansas College, started in 1850 in Fayetteville, was the first institution in the state to grant college degrees. Arkansas Industrial University, later renamed the University of Arkansas, opened in 1871 as a coeducational school. It has been the heart of the city ever since.

The university campus has a number of outstanding buildings. Its Old Main Building, completed in 1875, still dominates Fayetteville's skyline. The noted Arkansas architect Edward Durell Stone, a native of Fayetteville, designed its fine arts center. The Bud Walton Arena and the Walton Arts Center for the performing arts were both named for the family of Wal-Mart fame, who have contributed generously to the campus. The University of Arkansas is also the home of the renowned football and basketball teams called the Razorbacks. Just north of Fayetteville is Springdale, home of the giant poultry producers, Tyson Foods.

Old Main Building at the University of Arkansas

Eureka Springs is the most popular tourist destination in Arkansas after Hot Springs. During the late nineteenth century, like Hot Springs, it attracted visitors who believed that the spring waters had healing powers. They bathed in and drank the waters from the sixty-three springs, seeking cures for eye ailments, aches and pains in every part of the body, and various kinds of diseases. The first visitors arrived in wagons and carriages.

Basin Park Hotel in Eureka Springs

After the railroad came to town in 1883, the town became one of the most fashionable health spas in the United States. Elegant hotels and bathhouses sprang up. One of the most luxurious, the Crescent Hotel, is now being restored to its Victorian elegance.

Eureka Springs sits on an escarpment—a steep slope between two comparatively flat plateaus. It is so steep that the town's lowest street is more than 1,000 feet (305 m) below the highest. Eureka Springs has 230 streets, and it is said that no two of them intersect at right angles. One of its hotels, the Basin Park, has seven floors, and each floor has an outside entrance on the side of the hill. St. Elizabeth's Catholic Church is the only church in North America where the street-level entrance is through the bell tower at the top of the building.

Ozark Folk Center

The Ozark Folk Center State Park, opened in 1973 in Mountain View, is unlike any other state park. More than fifty buildings house an auditorium, a library, conference rooms, a restaurant, shops, and demonstration buildings. Artisans produce crafts with tools and methods used between 1820 and 1920. They demonstrate their skills for the public, making pottery, furniture, musical instruments, barrels and buckets, brooms, and baskets (above). The products are sold in the gift shop.

Many of the workers at the folk center follow the same traditions in their everyday life. They milk their own cows and churn their own butter. They raise sheep, then shear the wool, card, spin, and weave it into cloth. Most are local people. In a few cases, three generations of a family practice the same craft. Other people are outsiders who have come here to learn a traditional craft.

Music is another important part of the folk center. Concerts and dances are presented six nights a week. All the folk music performed is traditional, written before 1942 and played without amplification. ■

The Delta

Jonesboro is the largest town in northeastern Arkansas. It sits on Crowleys Ridge, with the delta on each side. Jonesboro is the site of Arkansas State University and the home of the world's largest rice mill.

Helena is known for its blues festivals.

Tucked between Crowleys Ridge and the Mississippi River is the town of Helena. Crowleys Ridge ends here—there are no hills on the west side of the river south of this point. The second incorporated town in the Arkansas Territory, Helena became an important port for the shipping of cotton when steamboats arrived in 1811. By the 1870s, it was also a railroad town, with as many as five trains a day. Mark Twain once called Helena the prettiest spot on the Mississippi. Several houses that survived the Civil War give Helena the appearance of a city of the Old South.

This is the blues center of Arkansas. The city has been known for the King Biscuit radio program since 1941. The annual King Biscuit Festival in October attracts more than 100,000 people.

Another annual treasure is the Warfield concert series. In 1967, a local farmer left an endowment to be used to present free concerts. A season's schedule includes a variety of music, such as opera, an international boys' choir, and a popular swing orchestra.

Stuttgart calls itself the "duck and rice capital of the world." It lies on the Grand Prairie, which is covered with topsoil on top of clay, making it ideal soil for growing rice. More than 103,500 acres (41,918 ha) in the region are planted in rice.

Craighead County

In the early years of the state, residents wanted to establish a new county in northeast Arkansas. Two state senators represented different factions. Senator William Jones led the movement to establish the new county while Senator Thomas Craighead opposed it. Jones waited until Craighead was absent one day, then called for a vote. His side won, and he generously suggested that the new county should be named Craighead, after the man who hadn't wanted it. Later the county seat was re-named Jonesboro, after Senator Jones. ■

On the Mississippi Flyway, thirty-seven varieties of ducks come through Stuttgart each year. The town hosts the World Championship Duck-Calling Contest during its Wings Over the Prairie Festival each November.

A vast, wild strip of bottomland hardwood forest east of Stuttgart is protected in the White River National Refuge. Considered one of the most important habitats for migratory waterfowl in the nation, it is also a haven for numerous songbirds and four-legged creatures.

Southern Arkansas

Geographers call the southern and southwestern part of the state the West Gulf Coastal Plain. The region is also called Timberlands.

Pine Bluff overlooks the Arkansas River about 110 miles (177 km) upstream from the Mississippi. A French farmer established a trading post there in 1819. The settlement developed into a prosperous river port, where cotton was shipped out from the

Picking cotton just north of Pine Bluff

Victims of World War II

In 1942, more than 110,000 people of Japanese descent were forcibly moved from their homes in western states and transported to ten scattered camps. Two of these camps, called "relocation centers" by the federal government but more realistically described as prison camps, were in southeastern Arkansas. About three-fourths of the Japanese people held here were American citizens, and the government action was a flagrant violation of their civil rights.

The two camps were located in Jerome and Rohwer. Each housed about 8,500 people. Living quarters were crudely and hastily built, the climate was hot and damp, and the ground was swampy, buggy, and full of deadly snakes.

Accounts by evacuees record that the local people were, for the most part, quite hostile and suspicious toward them. The bombing of Pearl Harbor had created a national atmosphere of antagonism against people with Asian features.

Toward the end of the war, the evacuees were moved out of Jerome, and a prison camp for German prisoners of war was established there. Ironically, those prisoners reported that their treatment was excellent. The site of the Rohwer center is now on the National Register of Historic Places. ■

---

delta. Cotton and lumber mills soon appeared. Today Pine Bluff, Arkansas's fourth-largest city, is an important agricultural and industrial center. Cotton and wood products are still processed here, along with soybeans, rice, and manufactured goods.

Downtown Pine Bluff is an outdoor art gallery. Murals that depict the history of the city and the region decorate the walls of many buildings, and more works are in progress.

El Dorado, close to the middle of the state's southern border, was the center of the oil boom in southern Arkansas. On January 10, 1921, a huge

Murals appear on many outdoor walls in Pine Bluff.

How Did They Get Those Names?

Smackover, Arkansas, probably got its name from a mispronunciation of the French name of a nearby bayou. The French words *sumac couvert,* meaning "covered way," could have been slurred into something sounding like "smackover." But some people claim the name came from the fabulous oil gusher that spewed oil "smack over" (all over) the area. It makes a better story, but it doesn't hold up, because the town had that name before the gusher came in.

Then there's the town of Toad Suck, on the Arkansas River near Conway. This story appears on a marker near the river landing: An early tavern keeper is said to have commented that riverboat workers who came into his bar would suck on beer bottles until their stomachs swelled up like toads. ■

geyser of oil gushed out of the ground. Within a few weeks, the sleepy little farming community exploded just as dramatically. The population grew from less than 4,000 to 25,000. The big oil field was a few miles north of town, near the smaller settlement of Smackover. For a few months in 1925, this was the biggest producing oil field in the United States. El Dorado was soon overrun by all kinds of lawless characters—gamblers, con men, moonshiners, and fortune hunters.

El Dorado is still the center of the Arkansas oil region, but its wild and lawless days are long past. Left behind is a legacy of impressive buildings dating from the 1920s and 1930s. The Arkansas Museum of Natural Resources is a state park 10 miles (16 km) north of the city. Huge derricks and other oil-drilling equipment are on display. A video and other exhibits tell the story of the region's exciting history.

Texarkana is a most unusual town. It lies right on the state line that separates Texas and Arkansas. The name is a combination of three state names: Texas, Arkansas, and Louisiana, which is 25 miles (40 km) south of the town. The post office here is the only one in the United States located in two states. Its official address is Texarkana, Arkansas-Texas.

One of Texarkana's most famous sons was Scott Joplin, the brilliant composer of ragtime music. An outdoor mural on a Main Street building illustrates his life and accomplishments.

A Texarkana wall mural that honors musician Scott Joplin

Hope is the small town a few miles northeast of Texarkana where President William Jefferson Clinton was born and attended school. The former railroad depot in the center of town is now a visitor center and museum.

One of Bill Clinton's two boyhood homes in Hope

CHAPTER SEVEN

Running the Government

Inside the state capitol

Arkansas has been governed under five state constitutions. The first was adopted in 1836, just before the state joined the Union. It was in effect until Arkansas joined the Confederacy during the Civil War.

A new document, known as the secession constitution, was adopted in 1861. Three years later, Union soldiers who were occupying Arkansas met in Little Rock with opponents of the Confederacy from some of the northern counties. They wrote a new, pro-federal constitution and declared the secession constitution null and void. Arkansas had two state constitutions, two governments, and two governors during the last year of the Civil War. Northern counties were generally pro-Union, while southern counties were usually pro-Confederacy.

During the Reconstruction Period, after the Civil War, Northerners moved into Arkansas to enforce the people's allegiance to the United States. These unwelcome outsiders were called "carpetbaggers" because they traveled with their belongings packed in pieces of luggage called carpetbags. A fourth constitution was adopted in 1868. Because of its extension of privileges to former slaves and restrictions imposed on former Confederates, this document became known as the carpetbag constitution.

Opposite: The state capitol

A crowd reacting to the Brooks–Baxter War

The Constitution of 1874

Election fraud was widespread during this difficult period. Economic conditions were harsh and the people were discontented with their government. Things reached a crisis when two Republicans, Joseph Brooks and Elisha Baxter, each claimed victory in the election for governor in 1872. The conflict, called the Brooks–Baxter War, ended when President Ulysses Grant declared Baxter the governor.

It was time for a new constitution, one that would help solve the state's problems and put an end to the evils of Reconstruction. The state legislature, in a special session, called a constitutional convention. In 1874, voters approved a new document containing nineteen articles.

Arkansas has been governed by the constitution of 1874 ever since. Conventions have met and proposed new constitutions in 1918, 1970, and 1980, but the voters defeated the proposals each time. Instead, the old document has been altered, patched, and amended dozens of times.

All five of the Arkansas constitutions have provided for the separation of governmental powers into three branches: the executive, legislative, and judicial. These provisions are like those in the federal constitution and in many other state constitutions.

The constitution of 1874 reflected a general attitude of keeping government weak. The legislature meets only once every two years, and sessions are restricted to sixty days unless an extension is approved by a two-thirds vote in each house. Until recently, most officials were elected for terms of only two years. An amendment approved in 1984 changed the length of terms to four years for the state's constitutional officers.

The state capitol in 1874

Voters must be citizens of the United States, must be at least eighteen years of age, and must register in their county of residence at least twenty days before an election. A voter's registration can be canceled for certain reasons, including failure to vote in any election during a four-year period.

Executive Branch

Voters elect seven state officers to serve for four-year terms: a governor, lieutenant governor, secretary of state, treasurer, auditor,

Arkansas's counties

attorney general, and commissioner of state lands. Candidates are allowed to run for no more than two consecutive terms.

Candidates for the offices of governor and lieutenant governor must be U.S. citizens, at least thirty years of age, and residents of Arkansas for seven years or more. The governor is the state's chief executive, top political officer, and representative of the state to the rest of the nation and the world.

The executive branch consists of 50 state departments and agencies and some 200 boards and commissions. These divisions of the executive branch regulate, supervise, and provide advice and assistance in many areas, including education, economic development, parks and tourism, highways, and health.

Arkansas's Governors

Name	Party	Term	Name	Party	Term
James Sevier Conway	Dem.	1836–1840	George Washington Donaghey	Dem.	1909–1913
Archibald Yell	Dem.	1840–1844			
Thomas S. Drew	Dem.	1844–1849	Joseph Taylor Robinson	Dem.	1913
John Seldon Roane	Dem.	1849–1852	George W. Hays	Dem.	1913–1917
Elias Nelson Conway	Dem.	1852–1860	Charles Hillman Brough	Dem.	1917–1921
Henry Massey Rector	Dem.	1860–1862	Thomas Chipman McRae	Dem.	1921–1925
Harris Flanagin (Confederate Governor)	Dem.	1862–1865	Thomas J. Terral	Dem.	1925–1927
			John Ellis Martineau	Dem.	1927–1928
Isaac Murphy (Union Governor)	Union	1864–1868	Harvey Parnell	Dem.	1928–1933
			Junius Marion Futrell	Dem.	1933–1937
Powell Clayton	Rep.	1868–1871	Carl E. Bailey	Dem.	1937–1941
Ozra A. Hadley	Rep.	1871–1873	Homer Martin Adkins	Dem.	1941–1945
Elisha Baxter	Rep.	1873–1874	Benjamin T. Laney	Dem.	1945–1949
Augustus Hill Garland	Dem.	1874–1877	Sidney Sanders McMath	Dem.	1949–1953
William R. Miller	Dem.	1877–1881	Francis Cherry	Dem.	1953–1955
Thomas J. Churchill	Dem.	1881–1883	Orval E. Faubus	Dem.	1955–1967
James Henderson Berry	Dem.	1883–1885	Winthrop Rockefeller	Rep.	1967–1971
Simon P. Hughes	Dem.	1885–1889	Dale L. Bumpers	Dem.	1971–1975
James Philip Eagle	Dem.	1889–1893	David H. Pryor	Dem.	1975–1979
William Meade Fishback	Dem.	1893–1895	Bill Clinton	Dem.	1979–1981
James P. Clarke	Dem.	1895–1897	Frank D. White	Rep.	1981–1983
Daniel Webster Jones	Dem.	1897–1901	Bill Clinton	Dem.	1983–1992
Jeff Davis	Dem.	1901–1907	Jim Guy Tucker	Dem.	1992–1996
John Sebastian Little	Dem.	1907–1909	Mike Huckabee	Rep.	1996–

Legislative Branch

Two houses make up the Arkansas general assembly—a senate of 35 members and a 100-member house of representatives. Senators serve staggered four-year terms, with half elected every two years. Representatives serve two-year terms. Senators must be at least twenty-five years of age, representatives at least twenty-one. All legislators must have lived in the state

The Arkansas house of representatives in session

for at least two years and in their districts for one year. The general assembly is responsible for passing laws to govern the state.

Judicial Branch

The judicial branch of government is made up of state and local courts. Judicial officers are responsible for enforcing the law as written in the state constitution and statutes.

The Arkansas court system consists of local courts, circuit and chancery courts, a court of appeals, and the Arkansas Supreme Court. All Arkansas judges hold elective office; none are appointed, as some judges are in other states. Salaries of court officials and court expenses are paid partly by the state and partly by local governments.

Arkansas is one of only three states that have two separate kinds of courts. Courts of law, or circuit courts, hear criminal cases and civil cases that involve damages. Courts of equity, or chancery courts, hear equity cases that do not involve monetary awards.

The Arkansas Supreme Court building

The State Flag and Seal

The Arkansas state flag was officially adopted by the general assembly in 1913. Its colors are the same as those of the U.S. flag—red, white, and blue. A large diamond with a blue border is imposed on a red background. Twenty-five white stars within the blue border stand for the fact that Arkansas was the twenty-fifth state to join the Union. In the center of the blue border is a diamond-shaped white field. A blue inscription, ARKANSAS, is printed across the center of this field. Three blue stars stand for Spain, France, and the United States, the three countries that owned the territory before it became a state. The white star commemorates the Confederacy. The diamond shape was chosen because Arkansas is a major diamond-producing state.

The official state seal (right), adopted in 1907, is filled with symbols: the Goddess of Liberty, the Angel of Mercy, the Sword of Justice, and an eagle holding a bundle of arrows in one claw and an olive branch in the other. Thirteen stars stand for the original thirteen states. Pictures on a shield stand for the state's heritage—a steamboat, a beehive, a plow, and a sheaf of wheat. A ribbon bears the state motto REGNAT POPULUS (*The People Rule*) and the circular border of the seal reads GREAT SEAL OF THE STATE OF ARKANSAS. ■

Arkansas Leaders in Washington

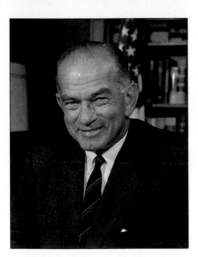

From 1945 to 1975, three of the most influential members of the U.S. Congress were from Arkansas. John L. McClellan (top left) served in the House of Representatives from 1935 to 1939, then in the Senate from 1943 to 1977. He was instrumental in getting federal funds to build flood-control dams and hydroelectric projects in his state. Fifteen artificial lakes were created in the process. He worked to fund a series of locks and dams on the Arkansas River. In 1971, the McClellan-Kerr Arkansas River Navigation System was dedicated, opening up the river to year-round traffic. McClellan gained national fame in the 1950s as chair of a congressional committee that conducted televised hearings on labor racketeering.

Wilbur D. Mills (center left) was elected to the House of Representatives in 1938 and held his seat until 1977. As chair of the powerful Ways and Means Committee, he gained a reputation for understanding the federal tax laws better than anyone else. He was often called the most influential man in Washington after the president. The most important legislation his committee produced was the Medicare Act of 1965.

J. William Fulbright (bottom right) had a distinguished career even before his thirty-two years in Congress. He was a football star at the University of Arkansas, a Rhodes scholar, and a law professor. Then at age thirty-four, he became president of his alma mater, one of the youngest university presidents in the nation.

Fulbright was elected to the House of Representatives a year later, served one term, and then moved to the Senate. During his thirty years in the Senate (1945–1975), Fulbright took an active interest in foreign affairs. He sponsored an act in 1946 to grant exchange scholarships to U.S. and foreign students. Thousands of people have been helped through Fulbright scholarships. While chair of the Senate Foreign Relations Committee, he was critical of the U.S. involvement in the Vietnam War.

Senator Fulbright was defeated in the 1974 election, partly because some voters felt he had not shown leadership in favor of civil rights. Like most Arkansas Democrats of their day, Fulbright, Mills, and McClellan had all declared opposition to the Brown desegregation decision by the Supreme Court. Years later, public opinion had changed. Together, the three Arkansans held elective office at the federal level for 108 years. ■

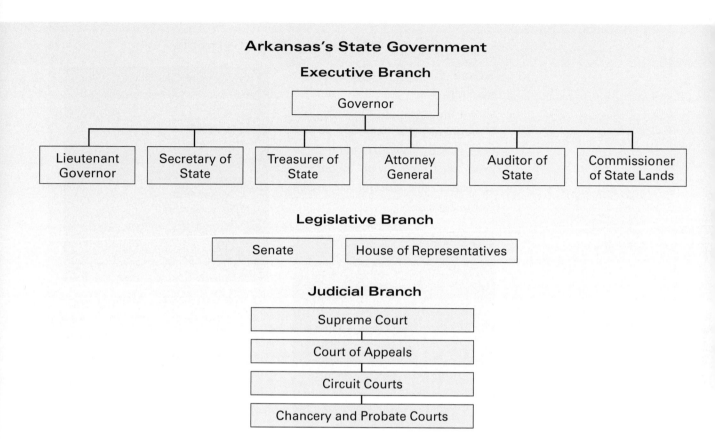

Arkansas's State Government

Executive Branch

Governor

Lieutenant Governor | Secretary of State | Treasurer of State | Attorney General | Auditor of State | Commissioner of State Lands

Legislative Branch

Senate | House of Representatives

Judicial Branch

Supreme Court

Court of Appeals

Circuit Courts

Chancery and Probate Courts

Local Government

Local governments in Arkansas consist of 75 counties and 481 active incorporated cities and towns. In general, they operate under laws passed by the general assembly. However, as of 1977, the counties have home rule and have certain specified powers as spelled out in an amendment to the state constitution.

Municipal governments, in general, do not have home rule. Some of their powers are granted by the constitution; others are controlled by the state legislature.

Arkansas's State Symbols

State flower: Apple blossom In 1901, the state general assembly designated the apple blossom as the state flower. At that time, Arkansas was a leading apple producer. The town of Lincoln still sponsors the annual Arkansas Apple Festival.

State insect: Honeybee The honeybee (above) was adopted as the state insect by the general assembly in 1973. An old-fashioned dome beehive is one of the symbols on the state seal of Arkansas.

State musical instrument: Fiddle The fiddle was adopted as the state instrument in 1985. The fiddle has long been commonly associated with Arkansas folk music and culture.

State gem: Diamond The diamond was adopted as Arkansas's state gem by the general assembly of 1967. Arkansas is the major diamond-producing state in the United States. The Crater of Diamonds State Park, located in

State bird: Mockingbird The mockingbird (above) was adopted as the state bird by the Arkansas legislature in 1929.

State tree: Southern pine Adopted in 1937, the loblolly and shortleaf pine varieties of the southern pine are found in the state's two national forests.

Murfreesboro, Arkansas, is the only place in the nation where you can dig for diamonds and keep what you find. More than 70,000 diamonds have been found there.

State beverage: Milk Milk was adopted as the Arkansas state beverage by the general assembly of 1985. Dairy farming is an important part of Arkansas agriculture.

State fruit and vegetable: South Arkansas vine-ripe pink tomato The South Arkansas vine-ripe pink tomato was adopted as the state fruit and vegetable in 1987. The tomato is officially defined as a fruit but is commonly used as a vegetable. The Pink Tomato Festival is held each year in Bradley County.

State American folk dance: Square dance The square dance was adopted as the state American folk dance by the general assembly in 1991. Square dancers perform a variety of steps that are usually called out during the dance by a person known as a square dance caller.

State mammal: White-tailed deer The white-tailed deer (above) was adopted as the state mammal by the general

assembly in 1993. The deer raises the white underside of its tail when frightened. Young white-tailed deer have a white-spotted red coat that changes to brownish gray before the end of its first year.

State rock: Bauxite Bauxite is a principal source of aluminum, which is used to make soft drink cans and aluminum foil. Saline County, Arkansas, is home to the largest bauxite deposits in the United States. Bauxite was adopted as the state rock in 1967.

State mineral: Quartz crystal Quartz crystals mined in the Ouachita Mountains are used in computers and sold to visitors. Sometimes called "Arkansas diamonds," quartz crystals are not true diamonds. The quartz crystal was adopted as the state mineral by the general assembly in 1967.

Arkansas's State Songs

Two songs were named official state songs in 1987 by the state general assembly: "Arkansas (You Run Deep in Me)" by Wayland Holyfield, and "Oh, Arkansas," by Terry Rose and Gary Klaff.

"Arkansas (You Run Deep in Me)"

October morning in the Ozark
   Mountains,
Hills ablazing like that sun in
   the sky.
I fell in love there and the fire's
   still burning
A flame that never will die.

Chorus:
Oh, I may wander, but when I
   do
I will never be far from you.
You're in my blood and I know
   you'll always be.
Arkansas, you run deep in me.
Moonlight dancing on a delta
   levee,

To a band of frogs and whip-
   poorwill
I lost my heart there one July
   evening
And it's still there, I can tell.

(Chorus)

Magnolia blooming, Mama
   smiling,
Mallards sailing on a December wind.
God bless the memories I keep
   recalling

(Chorus)

Like an old familiar friend.

(Chorus)

And there's a river rambling
   through the fields and
   valleys,
Smooth and steady as she
   makes her way south,
A lot like the people whose
   name she carries.
She goes strong and she
   goes proud.

(Chorus)

"Oh, Arkansas"

It's the spirit of the mountains
   and the spirit of the Delta,
It's the spirit of the Capitol
   dome.
It's the spirit of the river and
   the spirit of the lakes,
It's the spirit that's in each
   and every home.
It's the spirit of the people
   and the spirit of the land,
It's the spirit of tomorrow
   and today.

Chorus:
Oh Arkansas, Oh Arkansas,
   Arkansas U.S.A.
It's the spirit of friendship,
   it's the spirit of hope.
It's the Razorbacks every
   game they play.
Oh Arkansas, Oh Arkansas,
   Arkansas U.S.A.

It's the spirit of the forest, it's
   the spirit of the eagle.
It's the spirit of the country
   that we love.

It's the spirit of pride that we
   all feel deep inside,
It's the spirit that shines from above.
It's the spirit of our fathers,
   it's the spirit of our kids,
It's the spirit of the music that we
   play.

Oh Arkansas, Oh Arkansas,
   Oh Arkansas U.S.A.
Oh Arkansas, Oh Arkansas,
   Oh Arkansas U.S.A.
Oh Arkansas, Oh Arkansas,
   Oh Arkansas U.S.A.

Arkansas's State Anthem
"Arkansas"

I am thinking tonight of the
Southland,
Of the home of my childhood
days,
Where I roamed through the
woods and the meadows,
By the mill and the brook that
plays;
Where the roses are in
bloom,
And the sweet magnolia too,
Where the jasmine is white,
And the fields are violet blue,
There a welcome awaits all
her children

Who have wandered afar
from home.

Chorus:
Arkansas, Arkansas, 'tis a
name dear,
'Tis the place I call 'Home,
Sweet Home,'
Arkansas, Arkansas, I salute
thee,
From thy shelter no more I'll
roam.

'Tis a land full of joy and of
sunshine,

Rich in pearls and in diamonds rare,
Full of hope, faith, and love
for the stranger
Who may pass 'neath her
portals fair;
There the rice fields are full,
And the cotton, corn, and hay,
There the fruits of the field
bloom in winter months
and May,
'Tis the land that I love, first
of all dear,
And to her let us all give
cheer.

Civil Rights

In 1993, Arkansas became the forty-ninth state to pass a civil rights bill. It defines a citizen's rights of freedom from discrimination. It also sets forth procedures for bringing suit when those rights are violated. Citizens can bring suit when they believe they have been discriminated against because of "race, religion, ancestry or national origin, gender, or any . . . disability." This applies to discrimination in employment, use of public accommodations, property transactions, credit and contracts, and voting and participating in political processes.

CHAPTER EIGHT

Making a Living

Nearly 200 years ago, the frontier region that is now the state of Arkansas became part of the United States. For well more than half that time, most of the people of the region lived off the land. Those in the mountains hunted, fished, and grew crops on small farms. Planters in the delta acquired large tracts of land and grew cotton with the help of slave labor.

Agriculture Today

Today, about half the land area of Arkansas is used for agriculture. Rice and soybeans have replaced cotton as the state's most important crops. Arkansas is the largest producer of rice among the fifty states and the fourth-largest producer of cotton.

In terms of dollar value, the production of broilers, or chickens, for market brings in more than any of the crops. Tyson Foods, in Springdale, is the world's number-one food company based on

Soybeans are among the state's most important crops.

Opposite: A rice field near West Memphis

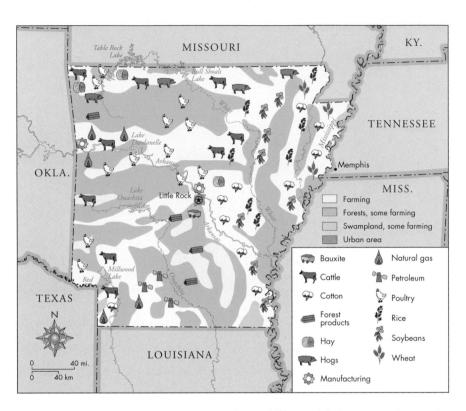

Arkansas's natural resources

Farming
Forests, some farming
Swampland, some farming
Urban area

Bauxite
Cattle
Cotton
Forest products
Hay
Hogs
Manufacturing

Natural gas
Petroleum
Poultry
Rice
Soybeans
Wheat

poultry. Tyson processes some 25 million chickens each week. The company employs about 12,000 people in northwest Arkansas. While Tyson is the giant, it is only one of many poultry processors in the state. Other companies also employ thousands of workers.

In 1994, the top ten agricultural products in Arkansas were broilers, soybeans, rice, beef cattle, cotton, eggs, turkeys, hogs, hay, and wheat.

Manufacturing

World War II marked a turning point in the economy of Arkansas. Beginning with the factories established here to turn out products needed for the war effort, Arkansas finally came into the Industrial

Sweet Potato Pie

This dessert has become common throughout the South, but it is especially popular in Arkansas's Ozark Mountains.

Ingredients:

- 1 1/2 pounds sweet potatoes
- 1 1/2 sticks soft margarine
- 2 cups sugar
- 3 eggs
- 15-oz. can of condensed milk
- 1/2 teaspoon ground ginger
- 1/2 teaspoon nutmeg
- 1/2 teaspoon ground cloves
- 1 tablespoon vanilla
- 1/2 cup milk
- a pinch of salt
- 1 frozen pie crust

Directions:

Wash the sweet potatoes, place in a large pot, and cover with water. Bring to a boil. Cook potatoes for about 45 minutes, or until soft. Drain and cool.

Peel potatoes and mash in a large bowl with margarine and sugar. Mix well. Beat the eggs separately, then add to mixture. Mix ingredients together, slowly stirring in spices and milk. Pour mixture into the frozen pie crust.

Bake in a 375°F preheated oven until center is firm.

Rice: From Paddy to Table

Two-thirds of the world's people depend on rice as a staple in their diet. Rice is grown in half a dozen states in the United States, but the leading producer is Arkansas.

Rice is grown on flooded land (above). In most other countries, rice farmers depend on seasonal rains to flood their fields, or rice paddies. In the United States, fields are surrounded by levees to keep the water in and are then flooded by irrigation. Before the fields are flooded, the seeds are sown either from airplanes or with the use of large grain-drilling equipment.

The fields remain flooded throughout most of the growing season. The grain needs the moisture, and the water also helps control weeds. Later, the water is drained off. Large combines are used to harvest the grain and separate it from the stalks. Then the rice is ready to go to the processing plant.

Next, the grain is placed in huge tanks and dried in warm air. The outer husks are removed. The remaining brown rice can be milled into two products—white rice and rice bran. Rice bran is used to add fiber and vitamins to many foods. Before the rice is ready for shipment, it must be sorted and carefully inspected to remove any broken or discolored grains. Forty different varieties of rice are grown in the United States. Think of the farms of Arkansas the next time you eat rice. ■

What Arkansas Grows, Manufactures, and Mines

Agriculture	Manufacturing	Mining
Chickens	Food products	Natural gas
Rice	Paper products	Petroleum
Soybeans	Wood products	
Cotton	Fabricated metal products	

Age. Industrialization developed over the next few decades. By the late 1980s, more than one-fourth of the state's workforce was employed in manufacturing. The major manufactured goods produced in Arkansas are chemicals, food products, lumber, paper, electric motors, furniture, home appliances, auto components, transformers, and apparel.

Lumbering has been an important industry in southern Arkansas for more than 100 years. The industry grew with the coming of railroads to the region. Unfortunately, early lumbering practices stripped timberlands bare, destroying wildlife habitats and causing soil erosion and floods.

After World War I, some of the lumber companies began to realize that more efficient forest management was needed to keep an ongoing supply of timber. They also began to make use of wood parts and by-products that had previously been wasted.

Even though the emphasis for employment in Arkansas has shifted from agriculture to manufacturing, the state's greatest wealth is still in the land—farms, forests, and mines. The processing of food, wood products, and minerals accounts for more than half the total value produced by the state's factories.

A lumber mill
processing pine logs

Mining

An important mineral called bauxite was discovered near Little Rock in 1887. Bauxite ore contains aluminum, a useful metallic element. It continues to be one of the state's important natural resources. Some of the ore is shipped out of state while some is manufactured locally into finished aluminum products.

Natural gas was produced near Fort Smith in 1901, and the first oil well in the state was drilled near El Dorado in 1921. It started a lucrative business and turned a few small villages in southern

Arkansas into overnight boomtowns. A number of working oil wells in that region are still producing. Mining is also important to the state, but it accounts for only about 1 percent of the total state product.

Mountain Valley Spring Water

Water from a natural spring in Hot Springs, Arkansas, has been enjoyed by celebrities since 1871. It was being served at the White House long before an Arkansas man moved there. Ever since Calvin Coolidge first served Mountain Valley Spring water in 1925, every succeeding president has appreciated its superior taste and purity.

The Mountain Valley Spring Company, founded in 1871, is one of Arkansas's oldest businesses. The bottling plant is located right at the spring, and every drop put into those bottles comes directly from the original source. This is the largest cold-water spring in the area.

Collections of antique bottles and historic photographs are housed in a company museum on Central Avenue in Hot Springs. ■

Sam Walton, Self-Made Billionaire

Young Sam Walton showed signs of unusual drive and ability at an early age. He worked hard to earn awards in scouting and became the youngest eagle scout in the state of Missouri. He was an honor-roll student and a state champion quarterback in high school. Besides those achievements, his fellow students elected him president of the student body. He was born in Oklahoma and educated in Missouri, but it was in Arkansas that Sam Walton found fame and fortune.

After graduating from the University of Missouri, Walton worked for J. C. Penney for a while. His first business venture, a Ben Franklin store in Newport, Arkansas, ended when he lost his lease. He was thirty-two years old at the time and was determined to succeed as a merchant. He moved to Bentonville and opened another small variety store, calling it Walton's 5 and 10. He and his brother were successful in opening several more small stores in other towns.

Sam Walton kept a sharp eye on what was happening in business. Soon he spotted a new trend in customers' buying habits—people were flocking to big discount stores in cities. The "five and dimes" that had been doing so well in small towns for years were beginning to fail. So he decided it was time to bring a discount store to a small town.

Sam and his brother opened the first Wal-Mart in Rogers on July 2, 1962. Within a year, the sales topped $1 million. Sam commented that his idea was paying off like an oil gusher. At first, Wal-Mart stores carried cheap items, but soon better-quality, brand-name items were added. The Waltons owned thirty stores by 1970, and from then on they just kept adding more stores. By the early 1990s, Wal-Mart sales were greater than those of the legendary Sears, Roebuck & Company.

When Sam Walton died in 1992, he left a huge fortune. At least four of his heirs are billionaires today, and his stores are known throughout the United States. ■

Service Industries

Transportation, communication, and public utilities account for about one-tenth of the state's gross domestic product and employ about 6 percent of the workforce. One trucking company, J. B. Hunt Transport, is the largest truckload carrier in the United States.

Nearly 23 percent of the state's workers have jobs in wholesale and retail trade. Two giants in retail trade—Wal-Mart stores and Dillard department stores—are headquartered in the state. Another nationally known Arkansas-based retail chain is TCBY (The Country's Best Yogurt) Enterprises.

Arkansas draws nature-loving tourists from all over.

Tourism

Arkansans are well aware that the state's natural recreational resources are among its greatest assets. Tourism has become more and more important to the economy.

The state has been especially active in expanding and promoting its system of state parks. The success and popularity of Petit Jean, the first state park (established in 1930), was an inspiration. By 1989, Arkansas had fifty-one state parks, twenty-nine of them with overnight facilities. They are well used by residents of the state, and they attract out-of-state tourists, as well.

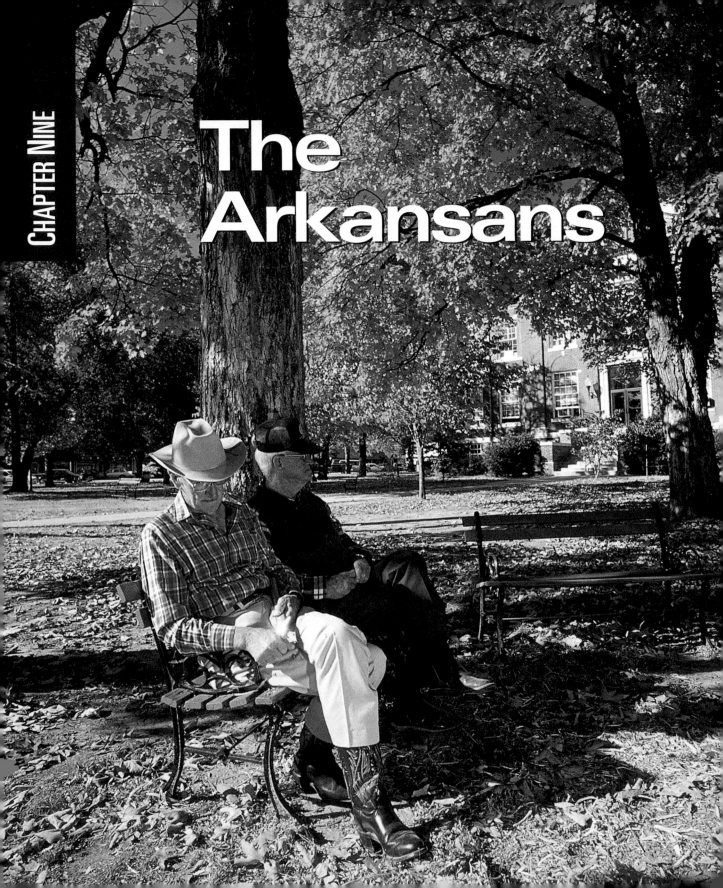

CHAPTER NINE

The Arkansans

The people of Arkansas are much more homogeneous— similar—than people in many other states. According to the 1990 census, about 83 percent of the state's residents were white, and most of them were of Irish, German, or English descent.

Almost 99 out of every 100 Arkansans were born in the United States. It is rare in Arkansas to meet someone who came from a foreign country. Arkansas has never had the large influx of immigrants that most industrial states have experienced.

At a dude ranch near Harrison

About 16 percent of the Arkansans are of African-American descent. This number has shrunk from about 40 percent since the 1940s.

The 1990 census counted 2,362,239 people in the state of Arkansas. It ranks thirty-third among the fifty states in population. Between 1940 and 1960, the state was losing in population; since then, the population has increased.

Arkansas has traditionally been a rural state. It is still much more rural than most of the United States (twice the national average), but that has been changing recently. Many residents have left farms and villages to work in the cities.

Opposite: Enjoying a warm day in Arkansas

Population of Arkansas's Major Cities (1990)

Little Rock	175,795
Fort Smith	72,798
North Little Rock	61,741
Pine Bluff	57,140
Jonesboro	46,535
Fayetteville	42,099

One-fourth of the population now lives in the ten largest cities—none of which, however, ranks among the nation's major cities in size. More than half of the people live in towns and cities of more than 5,000 people, classified as "urban" by the U.S. Census Bureau.

Northwest Arkansas is the fastest-growing section of the state. Some of the newcomers are retirees; others are young artists and independent entrepreneurs. In both cases, they have been attracted by the natural beauty, lower cost of living, and casual lifestyle of the region. Also, several thousand Hispanics have moved here to work in the chicken industry in and around Springdale. The population of the delta, on the other hand, has dropped.

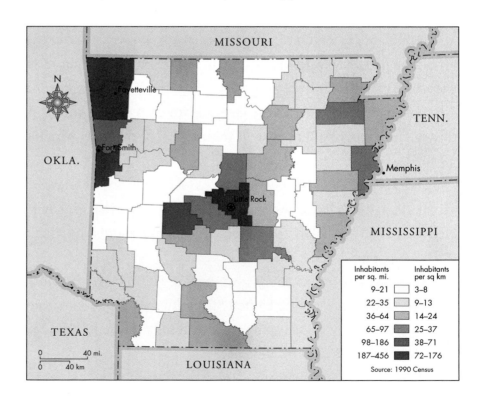

Arkansas's population density

Native Americans in Arkansas

Three major groups of Native Americans lived in Arkansas when the Europeans arrived—the Quapaw, Caddo, and Osage. The Quapaw and the Caddo were farmers. Peaceful people, they were governed by tribal elders and had good relations with their white neighbors. The Osage were nomadic hunters and less friendly to the settlers and explorers; their hunting bands and warriors roamed through the Ozarks.

When white settlers east of the Mississippi drove the Indians westward, a number of Cherokee came to the Arkansas Territory. They were farmers and had adopted much of the white settlers' lifestyle. The Cherokee settlement grew to more than 7,000 people. The Osage felt they were being invaded, but the Quapaw sided with the Cherokee.

But white settlers pressured the federal government to remove the Indians from the Arkansas Territory. The Quapaw were forced to give up their claims to millions of acres. During the 1820s, they were relocated to reservations in what is now Oklahoma.

Then in 1830, the U.S. Congress, with the approval of President Andrew Jackson, passed the Indian Removal Act. By 1836 there were almost no Native Americans left in Arkansas. ■

Religion

During the French and Spanish periods of Arkansas's early history, the official religion was Roman Catholicism. Catholic priests converted a number of the Native American leaders to their faith. After the United States acquired the Louisiana Territory, new settlers arrived from Tennessee, Mississippi, and other southern states. Baptist, Presbyterian, and Methodist missionary-preachers soon followed. Their efforts were rather slow to take effect. It is estimated that only about 17 percent of white Arkansans were church members by 1860.

In the northeastern states, churches were the backbone of two reform movements—

The state has churches of all denominations.

abolition, or antislavery, and temperance. Many devout Protestants in Arkansas were concerned about temperance, but almost no one raised a voice against slavery.

Strong divisions developed in some churches. Toward the end of the nineteenth century, a few new denominations, most of them conservative and evangelistic, gained membership in the state.

Today, much debate continues over religion in public schools. The most controversial subjects are the teaching of evolution and whether or not prayer and Bible reading should be permitted in public schools.

About two-thirds of the church members in Arkansas belong to Baptist and Methodist churches. Other major denominations are Roman Catholic, Presbyterian, Episcopal, Church of Christ, and Assembly of God.

Education

About 35 percent of the money spent by the state of Arkansas goes to support public and higher education. The first state governor, James Conway, spoke in his inaugural address about the need for a system of public schools. However, very little was done until after the Civil War.

Recent years have seen great improvement in public education in Arkansas. When he was governor, Bill Clinton made educational reform a major priority during his second administration. The program succeeded in decreasing the dropout rate for grades seven through twelve and increasing the number of students going on to college.

The number of public schools in Arkansas has decreased during the twentieth century because of consolidation. This trend has helped to raise the standards of education. At the same time, higher education has expanded.

There are ten public universities in the state, including five campuses of the University of Arkansas. In addition, there are several private colleges and universities, as well as twenty-three two-year community and technical colleges. The University of Arkansas at Fayetteville is especially noted for its work in physics research. World-class medical research is being carried out at the University of Arkansas for Medical Sciences in Little Rock.

Education has become a priority in Arkansas.

CHAPTER TEN

Enjoying Leisure Time

The people of Arkansas take pride in the natural beauty of their state. Whenever possible, great numbers of them head for the countryside. They use their beautiful rivers and lakes for boating, rafting, fishing, canoeing. They hike, drive, ride horseback, and bike in their many state parks. They climb the mountains and explore the underground caves.

But Arkansans also enjoy reading, listening to music, and admiring works of art. Quite a few of them have earned outstanding reputations in the arts.

And on Saturday afternoons in the fall, virtually the entire population of the state is focused on the latest accomplishments of the University of Arkansas football team—the mighty Razorbacks!

Camping along the Little Missouri River

Opposite: A friendly face from Arkansas

Frank Broyles

Frank Broyles was one of the most popular men in Arkansas during his years in Fayetteville. As head coach of the University of Arkansas football team, he led the Razorbacks to seven Southwest Conference championships and one national title. He won a whopping 70.7 percent of his games as coach.

Broyles was born in Georgia and graduated from Georgia Tech. An outstanding athlete in college, he won letters in three sports. He came to Arkansas after working as a university assistant coach at Baylor, Florida, and Georgia Tech, then as head coach at the University of Missouri. He was head coach of the Razorbacks from 1957 to 1976. In 1974, he was also named athletic director. ■

Sports

College football began in Arkansas in 1894, when the University of Arkansas formed a team called the Cardinals. In 1909, the team was renamed the Razorbacks. (Large numbers of wild pigs, called razorbacks, once roamed throughout the southeastern United States.)

Competitive sports grew in popularity as automobiles and roads made it possible for fans to drive to games. High school and college coaches of football and basketball became local heroes. One popular halfback at the university later became internationally famous as Senator William Fulbright.

Sports rapidly became the center of school life. Athletic events made education popular. Often other departments suffered, however, because funds were sometimes allocated for sports stadiums rather than libraries and laboratories.

The Razorbacks won their first Southwest Conference football championship in 1933. Over the next sixty-two years, they played in twenty-eight bowl games. Arkansas State University's football team, the Indians, has also produced quite a few all-American football players.

Meanwhile, the basketball Razorbacks have held their own. Six times since 1941, the team has reached National Collegiate Athletic Association (NCAA) Final Four standing. In 1994, the Razorbacks

Razorback basketball has been a national powerhouse over the years.

Scottie Pippen

Scottie Pippen was born in the tiny town of Hamburg, in southeastern Arkansas. He began to show his talent for basketball during his sophomore year at the University of Central Arkansas. In 1987, he became a member of the great Chicago Bulls basketball team. Chicago fans mourned the end of the fabulous era when Pippen helped win six national championships for their beloved Bulls. Besides regular-season play, Pippen was a member of the so-called Dream Team at the 1992 U.S. Olympics.

Pippen's teammate Michael Jordan was given much of the credit for leading the team to its six championships, but Bulls fans are well aware of the importance of Pippen and the rest of the team. Jordan and Pippen, backed up by the other players, moved about the basketball court as if it were a dance floor. Working as partners, always graceful and rhythmic, they made spectacular plays look easy.

In 1998, Scottie Pippen left Chicago to play with the Houston Rockets. In 1999, he was traded to the Portland Trailblazers. ■

defeated Duke University for the national championship. Several Razorback stars have gone on to play professional basketball.

The Arkansas Travelers is a double-A farm team of the St. Louis Cardinals. The baseball team is the state's only professional sports team. Local fans own and support the Travelers. The team has more than 1,200 stockholders.

Arkansas has produced quite a few athletic heroes over the years. Paul "Bear" Bryant, who died in 1983, was called "the winningest major-college football coach of all time." Sonny Liston won the world heavyweight boxing championship, then was defeated by Cassius Clay (now known as Muhammad Ali). Sidney Moncrief was a basketball star at the University of Arkansas. He went on to play professionally in Milwaukee, Wisconsin, where he was an NBA All-Star five times and was twice named Defensive Player of the Year.

Dozens of Arkansans are in the baseball record books. Among them are Hall-of-Famer "Dizzy" Dean and his brother Paul. Each of them pitched two of the winning four games of the 1934 World Series.

"Dizzy" Dean at spring training camp in 1935

Third baseman Brooks Robinson, also a Hall-of-Famer, played in five American League championships and four World Series. Preacher Roe, pitcher for the Dodgers, made it to the World Series three times.

The Arkansas Arts Council

The Arkansas Arts Council was established by the state legislature in 1971. Its programs encourage development of both performing and visual arts. County arts representatives work in each of the state's seventy-five counties.

The council helps to fund programs in the schools. The Arts in Education program sends dancers, musicians, actors, painters, writers, and sculptors to individual schools to perform and teach classes in their specialties. Arts on Tour sends performances and exhibitions to communities throughout the state. Individual artists are given grants and fellowships to help them pursue their professional goals.

The Arkansas Arts Center

The Arkansas Arts Center re-opened early in 2000, after extensive renovation and expansion. This busy center celebrates the visual and performing arts with a variety of exhibits and activities. Works by major artists, such as Rembrandt, Picasso, Pollock, Wyeth, and O'Keeffe, are among the museum's collections.

For children, the center offers a theater program and a studio school. Children's theater presentations are staged from September to April. A full-service restaurant and museum shop are part of the complex.

Two blocks away from the main building, a decorative arts museum is located in the large, historic home of Adolphine Terry. ■

Music

Arkansas has a rich legacy of traditional American music. Folk music has always been popular in the Ozarks. Folk music concerts are presented six nights a week from April through October at the Ozark Folk Center in Mountain View. The blues originated in the Mississippi Delta, and Helena is the Arkansas center for this kind of music.

A spring music festival in Little Rock features high-school marching bands from all over the state. One of America's greatest composers of ragtime music was Scott Joplin. He was born near Texarkana in 1868 and died in 1917. His compositions are still popular today.

Several Arkansans have been superstars of recorded music. Johnny Cash, the son of a sharecropper, was born in a three-room shack in Cleveland County. He has won eight Grammy awards. Glen Campbell, born in Delight and raised in nearby Billstown, has been successful in television and movies, as well as in popular music recording. Louis Jordan of Brinkley earned five gold records and is a member of the Rock and Roll Hall of Fame.

Johnny Cash was born in Cleveland County.

Opera singer Barbara Hendricks

Arkansan Barbara Hendricks is a distinguished opera singer. She has performed at the Metropolitan Opera in New York, the Paris Opera, and Italy's La Scala. She also performed at President Clinton's first inauguration.

William Warfield, actor and Grammy-winning singer, was born in West Helena. Although he lived in Arkansas for only a short time, he has called himself a "child of Arkansas" because of his parents' background. He is well known for his roles in *Show Boat, Green Pastures,* and *Porgy and Bess.*

Novelist John Grisham

Literature

Several dozen Arkansas writers published novels during the twentieth century. The most successful of them all, in terms of sales, is John Grisham. His legal thriller novels sell in the millions and are quickly made into popular movies. Another prolific writer from the state is Joan Hess, whose books sometimes have Arkansas settings.

Maya Angelou was brought up in the little town of Stamps,

Dee Brown

Dee Brown was five years old when his family moved from Louisiana to Arkansas. Soon after that, his grandmother taught him to read. He fell in love with printed words—in newspapers, magazines, and books. Reading was his main source of entertainment in those days before radio and television were common household equipment. He read his way through much of the local library collection.

Brown went to work for a small-town newspaper soon after he finished high school. Before long, he decided he wanted more education and enrolled in Arkansas State Teachers College. He worked part-time in the college library. His love of books continued to grow, and he decided to become a librarian.

Dee Brown is the author of more than two dozen books, but he always regarded his writing as a hobby. His career, he insisted, was his library work.

As a student of history, Brown was especially interested in the development of the American West. His best-selling book, *Bury My Heart at Wounded Knee,* is a hard-hitting saga of the war waged by the U.S. government against Native Americans.

Brown returned to live in Arkansas after his retirement from the faculty of the University of Illinois. In 1993, he published his memoirs in a book called *When the Century Was Young.* ■

near Magnolia, where she helped her grandmother run a general store. She has been successful in several fields—professional dancing, acting, writing, and teaching. She has won both Tony and Emmy awards for her acting. Her books have been nominated for the Pulitzer Prize and the National Book Award. Dr. Angelou frequently lectures on literature for educational TV.

Maya Angelou spent much of her childhood in the town of Stamps.

Thorncrown Chapel

A tiny, but famous, structure is almost hidden from view on a hillside near Eureka Springs. All the walls are built of glass supported by beams of natural wood. The beams thrust upward toward a peaked roof, forming a geometric grid of triangles and diamonds. Surrounded by woods, the chapel is only a short uphill walk from a busy highway.

Thorncrown Chapel is nondenominational and open year-round for meditation and prayer. The simplicity of its glass design draws a person's attention outward to the natural setting. Nothing obstructs the views of changing seasons on the wooded slope around it. The highway below seems far away.

The American Institute of Architects (AIA) named Thorncrown Chapel, designed by architect E. Fay Jones, the best American building of the 1980s. ■

President Clinton invited Maya Angelou to take part in his first inauguration ceremony. She wrote and read an original poem for the occasion. Angelou's autobiographical book *I Know Why the Caged Bird Sings* is a vivid description of what life was like for blacks in segregated Arkansas.

Visual Arts

Arts and crafts fairs are popular in Arkansas, and both Hot Springs and Eureka Springs are well-known artists' colonies. Recently, both these cities have sponsored street-painting festivals to encourage the creativity of both young and old artists.

Traditional Arkansas crafts often reach a high level of artistry. The Arkansas Crafts Guild has several hundred members. Some of their best work is sold in their galleries in Mountain View and three other locations around the state. Many of the quilts, pottery, wooden objects, and various decorative arts are of museum quality.

A native of Fayetteville established an international reputation in architecture. Edward Durell Stone, born in 1902, lived in Arkansas until he was a young man. He dropped out of the University of Arkansas and moved to Boston, where he attended both Harvard and MIT. Though he never earned an academic degree, his talent brought him commissions to design great buildings. Among them were the U.S. Embassy in New Delhi, India; the John F. Kennedy Center for

Edward Durell Stone was a well-known architect.

Matt Bradley

Donald Matthew (Matt) Bradley Jr., of Little Rock, has turned a high-school hobby into a profession and a fine art.

Matt Bradley grew up in Pine Bluff, Arkansas. A good student, he was admitted to the U.S. Air Force Academy in Colorado Springs, where he majored in engineering management. Following military pilot training, he hoped that being in the Air Force would give him opportunities to fly and to see the world.

"I joined the Air Force to fly," he says. However, Captain Bradley soon found himself spending more time working on the base newspaper than in the cockpit. A military photographer taught him how to develop and print pictures.

Before long, Bradley left the Air Force and began traveling all over Arkansas with his camera. His first professional assignment, to photograph the Buffalo National River for the National Geographic Society, led to a twenty-five-year career as a freelance photographer and writer. His latest book, co-authored with his wife, Susan, and titled *The Gift,* involved travel to eighteen countries. ■

the Performing Arts in Washington, D.C.; and several buildings on the University of Arkansas campus. Stone's autobiography was published in 1962; he died in 1978.

Another Arkansas architect, E. Fay Jones, is internationally famous for his nondenominational Thorncrown Chapel, near Eureka Springs. In 1990, President George Bush presented Jones with the American Institute of Architects' (AIA) Gold Medal for Lifetime Achievement.

The Future

Arkansas has a strong and beautiful tradition of independence, self-reliance, and respect for tradition. It also produces leaders who

search for ways to move forward with confidence. Both elements are important. The challenge is to find paths of progress without discarding the values of heritage.

Arkansas has much to expect from its future.

The Natural State is one of the loveliest in the nation. It has produced some brilliant leaders. Its citizens enjoy living here, and many who visit decide to stay. There is every reason to expect a bright future for Arkansas.

Timeline

United States History

The first permanent English **1607**
settlement is established in North
America at Jamestown.

Pilgrims found Plymouth Colony, the **1620**
second permanent English settlement.

America declares its independence **1776**
from Britain.

The Treaty of Paris officially ends the **1783**
Revolutionary War in America.

The U.S. Constitution is written. **1787**

The Louisiana Purchase almost **1803**
doubles the size of the United States.

The United States and Britain **1812–15**
fight the War of 1812.

The North and South fight **1861–65**
each other in the American Civil War.

Arkansas State History

1541 De Soto crosses the Mississippi into
present-day Arkansas.

1682 France claims ownership of the land
drained by the Mississippi River,
including Arkansas.

1803 President Thomas Jefferson purchases
Arkansas as part of the Louisiana
Purchase.

1817 Fort Smith is built as a military outpost.

1819 The *Arkansas Gazette*, the first newspaper west of the Mississippi, is founded.

1821 The state capital moves to Little Rock.

1836 The state of Arkansas joins the Union.

1868 Arkansas rejoins the Union after the
Civil War.

1874 Arkansas adopts a constitution.

United States History

The United States is involved **1917–18**
in World War I.

The stock market crashes, **1929**
plunging the United States into
the Great Depression.

The United States **1941–45**
fights in World War II.

The United States becomes a **1945**
charter member of the U.N.

The United States **1951–53**
fights in the Korean War.

The U.S. Congress enacts a series of **1964**
groundbreaking civil rights laws.

The United States **1964–73**
engages in the Vietnam War.

The United States and other **1991**
nations fight the brief
Persian Gulf War against Iraq.

Arkansas State History

1909 Arkansas establishes its first board of
education.

1921 The southern Arkansas oil boom
begins.

1930s The Civilian Conservation Corps
develops Petit Jean State Park.

1932 Arkansas becomes the first state to
elect a woman to the U.S. Senate.

1942 The U.S. government establishes
"relocation camps" for people of
Japanese descent in Jerome and
Rohwer.

1957 Governor Orval Faubus calls in the
National Guard to prevent black
students from attending Central
High School.

1978 Arkansans elect Bill Clinton as
governor of Arkansas.

1992 Americans elect Bill Clinton president
of the United States.

Fast Facts

State capitol

Statehood date	June 15, 1836, the 25th state
Origin of state name	French variant of a *Quapaw* term meaning "land of the downstream people"
State capital	Little Rock
State nickname	The Natural State; Land of Opportunity
State motto	*Regnat Populus* (The People Rule)
State bird	Mockingbird
State flower	Apple blossom
State tree	Southern pine
State insect	Honeybee
State rock	Bauxite
State mineral	Quartz crystal
State gem	Diamond
State fruit and vegetable	South Arkansas vine-ripe pink tomato

Digging for diamonds

A craft worker

State mammal	White-tailed deer
State musical instrument	Fiddle
State beverage	Milk
State American folk dance	Square dance
State songs	"Arkansas (You Run Deep in Me)" and "Oh, Arkansas"
State anthem	"Arkansas"
State fair	Little Rock (late September–early October)
Total area; rank	53,183 sq. mi. (137,744 sq km); 28th
Land; rank	52,076 sq. mi. (134,877 sq km); 27th
Water; rank	1,107 sq. mi. (2,867 sq km); 25th
Inland water; **rank**	1,107 sq. mi. (2,867 sq km); 18th
Geographic center	Pulaski, 12 miles (19 km) northwest of Little Rock
Latitude and longitude	Arkansas is located approximately between 33° and 36° 30' N and 89° 04' and 94° 42' W
Highest point	Magazine Mountain, 2,753 feet (840 m)
Lowest point	55 feet (17 m) above sea level at Ouachita River
Largest city	Little Rock
Number of counties	75
Population; rank	2,362,239 (1990 census); 33rd
Density	44 persons per sq. mi. (17 per sq km)
Population distribution	53% urban, 47% rural

Wildflowers

Ethnic distribution (does not equal 100%)	
White	82.73%
African-American	15.91%
Hispanic	0.85%
Native American	0.54%
Asian and Pacific Islanders	0.53%
Other	0.29%

Record high temperature	120°F (49°C) at Ozark on August 10, 1936
Record low temperature	–29°F (–34°C) at Benton County on February 13, 1905
Average July temperature	81°F (27°C)
Average January temperature	40°F (4°C)
Average annual precipitation	49 inches (124 cm)

Natural Areas and Historic Sites

National Park
Hot Springs National Park preserves forty-seven thermal springs.

National Memorial
Arkansas Post National Memorial is the site of the first permanent French settlement in the Lower Mississippi Valley (1686).

National River
Buffalo National River preserves one of the last free-flowing rivers in the lower forty-eight states.

National Historic Site
Fort Smith National Historic Site contains an early U.S. military post that was established to control American Indians.

Stairstep Falls along the Buffalo River

Petit Jean Mountain

National Military Park
Pea Ridge National Military Park is the site of an important Union victory in 1862 during the Civil War.

National Forests
Three national forests are located in Arkansas covering approximately 2.4 million acres (920,000 ha). The largest national forest in Arkansas is Ouachita National Forest. Parts of this forest lie in Oklahoma. Within this forest is Caddo Gap, where Spanish explorer Hernando de Soto was the first European to explore the area.

State Parks
Arkansas has 51 state parks that provide a wide range of recreational and wilderness experiences.

Sports Teams
NCAA Teams (Division 1)
Arkansas State University Indians

University of Arkansas Fayetteville Razorbacks

University of Arkansas Little Rock Trojans

Cultural Institutions
Libraries
The University of Arkansas in Fayetteville has the state's largest book collection.

Museums
The University of Arkansas Museum (Fayetteville) contains both historical and archaeological exhibits and artifacts.

Arkansas's First State Capitol (Little Rock) has been restored and now serves as a historical museum.

Arkansas Museum of Science and History (Little Rock) has an interesting mix of exhibits on history and science.

The Hampson Museum (Wilson) exhibits a fine collection of artifacts from the Mound Builder period.

Razorbacks

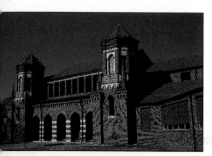

Bentonville High School

Universities and Colleges
In the late 1990s, Arkansas had 26 public and 12 private institutions of higher learning.

Annual Events

January–March
Thoroughbred racing at Oaklawn Park in Hot Springs
  (late January–April)

Jonquil Festival in Old Washington State Park (March)

Easter Sunrise Service in Hot Springs (Easter Sunday)

April–June
Arkansas Folk Festival and Arkansas Craft Guild Spring Show
  in Mountain View (April)

Back-in-the-Hills Antique Show and Crafts Fair in War Eagle (May)

Quapaw Quarter Tour of historic homes in Little Rock (May)

Riverfest in Little Rock (May)

Arkansas–Oklahoma Rodeo in Fort Smith (June)

Music Festival of Arkansas in Fayetteville (June)

Miss Arkansas Pageant in Hot Springs (June)

Pink Tomato Festival in Warren (June)

Old Fort Days Rodeo and River Festival in Fort Smith (June)

July–September
Peach Festival in Clarksville (July)

Rodeo of the Ozarks in Springdale (July)

White River Water Carnival in Batesville (August)

Greers Ferry Lake Water Festival in Heber Springs (August)

Hope Watermelon Festival (August)

Arkansas State Fiddlers' Championship in Mountain View
  (September)

A dude ranch in Harrison

Antique Car Festival in Eureka Springs (September)

Four States Fair and Rodeo in Texarkana (September)

Wine Festival in Altus (September)

October–December

Ozark Frontier Trail Festival and Craft Show in Heber Springs (October)

Ozark Folk Center Family Harvest Festival in Mountain View (October)

Ozarks Arts and Crafts Fair in War Eagle (October)

National Wild Turkey Calling Contest and Turkey Trot Festival in Yellville (October)

Rice Festival in Weiner (October)

Original Ozark Folk Festival in Eureka Springs (late October or early November)

Arts, Crafts, and Design Fair in Little Rock (November)

World's Championship Duck-Calling Contest in Stuttgart (November)

Arkansas Territorial Restoration Christmas Open House in Little Rock (December)

Famous People

Johnny Cash

Johnny Cash (1932–)	Singer
William Jefferson (Bill) Clinton (1946–)	U.S. president
Jay Hanna (Dizzy) Dean (1911–1974)	Baseball player
Orval Faubus (1910–)	Governor
John Johnson (1918–)	Publisher
Scott Joplin (1868–1917)	Musician and composer
Douglas MacArthur (1880–1964)	Soldier and statesman
Edward Durell Stone (1902–1978)	Architect

To Find Out More

History

- Di Piazza, Domenica. *Arkansas*. Minneapolis: Lerner Publications, 1994.

- Fradin, Dennis Brindell. *Arkansas*. Chicago: Childrens Press, 1994.

- Kelso, Richard. *Days of Courage: The Little Rock Story*. Austin, Tex.: Raintree/Steck-Vaughn, 1993.

- Love, Berna. *Arkansas Indians: Learning and Activity Book*. Little Rock: August House, 1996.

- Thompson, Kathleen. *Arkansas*. Austin, Tex.: Raintree/Steck-Vaughn, 1996.

Biography

- Beals, Melba Pattillo. *Warriors Don't Cry: A Searing Memoir of the Battle to Integrate Little Rock's Central High*. New York: Washington Square Press, 1994.

- Greene, Carol. *Bill Clinton: Forty-Second President of the United States*. Danbury, Conn.: Children's Press, 1997.

- Shapiro, Miles. *Maya Angelou*. Broomall, Penn.: Chelsea House, 1994.

Fiction

- Branscum, Robbie. *Johnny May*. Garden City, N.Y.: Doubleday, 1975.

- Branscum, Robbie. *Toby, Granny, and George*. Garden City, N.Y.: Doubleday, 1976.

- Crofford, Emily. *A Place to Belong*. Minneapolis: Carolrhoda Books, 1994.

Website
- **State of Arkansas**
  http://www.state.ar.us/
  The official website for the state of Arkansas

Addresses
- **Department of Parks and Tourism**
  1 Capitol Mall
  Little Rock, AR 72201
  For information about travel in Arkansas

- **Secretary of State's Office**
  Information Services
  State Capitol
  Little Rock, AR 72201
  For information about Arkansas's history and government

- **Arkansas Industrial Development Commission**
  1 Capitol Mall
  Little Rock, AR 72201
  For information about Arkansas's economy

Index

Page numbers in *italics* indicate illustrations.

Meet the Author

Sylvia McNair was born in Korea and grew up in Vermont. She believes she inherited a love of travel from her missionary parents. After graduating from Oberlin College, she held a variety of jobs, married, had four children, and settled in the Chicago area. She now lives in Evanston, Illinois. She is the author of several travel guides and nearly two dozen books for young people published by Children's Press.

"When I first visited Arkansas, many years ago, I came home with memories of hills and woods, lakes and rivers, and a beautiful camping trip in Hot Springs National Park. Since then I have traveled to many parts of the state, and I'm always impressed with its never-ending variety. Its beauty, its music, its arts and crafts, and its friendly people draw me back again and again.

"Writing a book about a specific state or country gives me the chance to learn as much as I can about the subject. I read, interview people, and see what I can find on the Internet. When I'm reading or writing about a particular place, I'm really there, in my imagination.

Each state has its own history, landscape, and personality. I hope this book will give young people a desire to learn more about Arkansas."

McNair has traveled in all fifty states and more than forty other countries. "Every place has its own story, and wherever I am, I find something to enjoy and appreciate."

Photo Credits